OTHER VOLUMES IN THIS SERIES

John Ashbery, editor, *The Best American Poetry 1988*

Donald Hall, editor, *The Best American Poetry 1989*

Jorie Graham, editor, *The Best American Poetry 1990*

Mark Strand, editor, *The Best American Poetry 1991*

Charles Simic, editor, *The Best American Poetry 1992*

Louise Glück, editor, *The Best American Poetry 1993*

A. R. Ammons, editor, *The Best American Poetry 1994*

Richard Howard, editor, *The Best American Poetry 1995*

Adrienne Rich, editor, *The Best American Poetry 1996*

James Tate, editor, *The Best American Poetry 1997*

Harold Bloom, editor, *The Best of the Best American Poetry 1988–1997*

John Hollander, editor, *The Best American Poetry 1998*

Robert Bly, editor, *The Best American Poetry 1999*

Rita Dove, editor, *The Best American Poetry 2000*

Robert Hass, editor, *The Best American Poetry 2001*

Robert Creeley, editor, *The Best American Poetry 2002*

THE
BEST
AMERICAN
POETRY
2003

◇ ◇ ◇

Yusef Komunyakaa, Editor

David Lehman, Series Editor

SCRIBNER POETRY

NEW YORK LONDON TORONTO SYDNEY SINGAPORE

SCRIBNER POETRY
1230 Avenue of the Americas
New York, NY 10020

SCRIBNER POETRY *and design are trademarks*
of Macmillan Library Reference USA, Inc., used under license
by Simon & Schuster, the publisher of this work.

For information about special discounts for bulk purchases,
please contact Simon & Schuster Special Sales:
1-800-456-6798 or business@simonandschuster.com

Text set in Bembo

Manufactured in the United States of America

1 3 5 7 9 10 8 6 4 2

Library of Congress Cataloging-in-Publication Data is available.

ISBN 0-7432-0387-9
0-7432-0388-7 (Pbk)
ISSN 1040-5763

CONTENTS

THE
BEST
AMERICAN
POETRY
2003

David Lehman was born in New York City in 1948. He is the author of five books of poems, including *The Daily Mirror* (2000) and *The Evening Sun* (2002), both from Scribner. Among his nonfiction books are *The Last Avant-Garde: The Making of the New York School of Poets* (Anchor, 1999) and *The Perfect Murder* (Michigan, 2000). He edited *Great American Prose Poems: From Poe to the Present,* which appeared from Scribner in 2003. He teaches writing and literature in the graduate writing programs of New School University in New York City and Bennington College in Vermont, and offers a course on "Great Poems" in the undergraduate honors program at NYU. He initiated *The Best American Poetry* series in 1988 and received a Guggenheim Fellowship a year later. He lives in New York City.

FOREWORD

by David Lehman

◊   ◊   ◊

On being named the official state poet of Vermont in 1961, Robert Frost acknowledged the honor in epigrammatic verse. "Breathes there a bard who isn't moved, / When he finds his verse is understood," he wrote, declaring himself happy to have won the approval of his old "neighborhood." Twenty-five years later, the position that had dowdily been called Poetry Consultant to the Library of Congress—a position that Frost had held when Dwight Eisenhower was president—received a major upgrade in title. It was to be the same nondescript job (give a reading, give a speech, answer the mail) but henceforth the person would be called U. S. Poet Laureate. The change of name proved prophetic, for the post soon acquired a high prestige. Joseph Brodsky kicked off his tenure in 1992 with a memorable speech proposing that poetry books be sold at checkout counters and provided in hotel rooms beside the Bibles and phone directories. Robert Pinsky, who served three one-year terms as laureate, became a familiar face reading poems on the PBS evening news, and he remains a cultural celebrity. (In 2002, he turned up in Jane Leavy's acclaimed biography of Dodger southpaw Sandy Koufax and in an episode of *The Simpsons,* where he gives a reading at a campus coffee shop surrounded by frat boys who have the name of Japanese haiku poet Bashō—mentioned in the opening lines of Pinsky's poem "Impossible to Tell"—painted on their bare chests.) Billy Collins, the current poet laureate, addressed a special joint session of Congress in Lower Manhattan a day before the first anniversary of September 11, 2001. "The Names," the fifty-four-line elegy he read, appeared in its entirety in the *New York Times.* When Collins, whose books are best-sellers, paid a recent visit to a grade school, one awestruck pupil inquired about the presidential line of succession: "How many people have to die before you can become president?"

It now seems that most of the states, many cities, and even a number of boroughs have or want to have their own official laureates. The appointments have proliferated. Though with Whitman and Mark Twain as our mainstays we may remain a little leery of titles, ranks, dukes, and airs, we also seem to revel in some of these things, and we put a value on the ceremonial and public uses of poetry that come with the territory. Not all the appointees rise to the occasion with the laconic wit and grace of Robert Frost, but neither had anyone done harm or caused a furor until last year. Within a month of being named the poet laureate of New Jersey, Amiri Baraka took part in the wildly popular Geraldine R. Dodge Poetry Festival in Stanhope, New Jersey. The observances surrounding the first year anniversary of September 11 were still fresh in people's minds when Baraka—the former LeRoi Jones—read "Somebody Blew Up America," a poem he had written about that atrocious day. These lines made listeners gasp: "Who knew the World Trade Center was gonna get bombed / Who told 4,000 Israeli workers at the twin towers / To stay at home that day / Why did Sharon stay away?" An avid Internet user, Baraka had given credence to a paranoid conspiracy theory that had spread with the speed of electronic spam. In actuality, seven Israelis died in the attacks, two on a hijacked plane and the rest in the Twin Towers, in addition to the many American Jews that perished on September 11. But Baraka had not subjected his poem to a fact-checking test. In interviews he thumbed his nose in doggerel and puns: "It's not a bad thing to be attacked by your enemies. It shows, obviously, that you don't need an enema yet."

As only the second poet laureate in New Jersey history, Baraka benefited from a quirk in the legislation that created the position but failed to specify how a laureate may be discharged or removed. Since Governor James McGreevey couldn't fire him and since he wouldn't resign, the New Jersey state legislature moved to abolish the post of poet laureate altogether. Never did a bill pass through committee so swiftly. Did this demonstrate that poetry is the first casualty of any controversy involving it? Or did it show up Baraka as an aging ego-tripper, who would opt to see the laureateship abolished—and other poets thereby punished— sooner than withdraw his anti-Semitic smear? The satirical newspaper *The Onion* refused to lose its sense of humor. A headline in the October 17–23, 2002, issue declared "Nantucket Poet Laureate Refuses to Apologize for Controversial Limerick." That the headline referred the reader to page 3C, where there was no story, seemed part of the point. Satirical wit involves not the letting loose of calumny but the telling of truths that liars deny, euphemisms hide, and platitudes obscure. In a subsequent issue *The Onion* displayed the kind of fearless humor that makes for a badly needed corrective to sentimentality and "correctness" (always a version of sentimentality) in the reception of poetry. The story of a wheelchair-bound author of best-selling inspirational verse ran under the heartless headline "Nation Afraid to Admit 9-Year-Old Disabled Poet Really Bad."

The widespread notice of an incendiary or scandalous poem—and more than one such surfaced last year—made for intense conversation. Liam Rector, in his column in *American Poetry Review,* asked whether we should regard poems as "works of fiction protected from accountable, verifiable reality by their imaginative basis" or as "works of nonfiction, which abide by an infinitely different set of expectations, rules, and accountability"? Good question. And there are others that poets are debating. What are the author's responsibilities? When does poetic speech become public speech that is subject to a truth-telling standard? Just how does one write about a world historical event on the order of 9/11? While there is no set answer to any of these questions, there are honorable ways to respond to the last of them. Several were chosen for *The Best American Poetry 2003.* A number of other poems in this volume bravely address issues of urgent immediacy. It could be that the inflection of this urgency, whether the subject matter be frighteningly near (terrorism in ghastly deed and threat) or merely eternal (the effect of death on the living, the image of a man running), is what distinguishes this year's edition of the anthology. The press of reality affects poets in diverse ways, and for some, the urge to write about events of great moment amounts to a moral imperative. This impulse is as understandable as it is difficult to resist and, when done with intelligence and skill, admirable. It seems to me, however, that something should also be said for the opposite impulse: the reluctance to speak hastily, the refusal to address a subject, any subject, that the writer himself or herself does not wish to address, or feel able to address. Isn't this a dimension of poetic license? The poets' freedom in regard to subject matter includes the freedom of reticence, whether it originates in the belief that the subordination of poetry to politics proves injurious to the former while leaving the latter unscathed, or whether it follows from the conviction that "the deepest feeling always shows itself in silence" (Marianne Moore). Declining an editor's summons for newly minted verse a few weeks after September 11, Richard Wilbur sent this terse response: "The only thing I can say right now is this. There is no excuse for the cold inhumanity of 11 September, and there is no excuse for those Americans, whether of the left or the religious right, who say that we had it coming to us."

Many poets have rediscovered, with exhilaration, a sense of political purpose in the past year. During the feverish days in February 2003 when the United States prepared its military for war with Iraq, thousands of protesting poets registered their indignation in verse. The emergence of poets and artists "trying to recapture their place as catalysts for public debate and dissent" became itself a part of the media story, though by no means as hotly controversial as the phenomenon of "celebrity activists" such as Martin Sheen or Janeane Garofalo. When Laura Bush invited hundreds of American poets to the White House for a symposium on Whitman, Dickinson, and Langston Hughes, a protest initiated by Sam Hamill, the poet and publisher of Copper Canyon Press, made the First Lady think twice, and the event was canceled. (Here was proof, one scribe sourly noted, that "the most effective poetry reading is the one that never happens.") The anti-war poem, a genre moribund since the last helicopter lifted off a Saigon rooftop in 1975, gained a new currency. Thousands of protest poems were produced, published, or posted. Whether the work had any merit seemed to be beside the point, and that is an oddity of the phenomenon. Self-styled poems of conscience make the peculiar demand that we suspend our faculty of critical discrimination. In February 2003 a seven-line poem entitled "The Bombs" by the British dramatist Harold Pinter—who has written superb plays and screenplays—was printed on page one of London's *Independent*. Here is the poem complete: "There are no more words to be said / All we have left are the bombs / Which burst out of our head / All that is left are the bombs / Which suck out the last of our blood / All we have left are the bombs / Which polish the skulls of the dead." Tired language, mixed metaphors, incoherent imagery: whatever it may have done to rally or reflect public opinion in Britain, this is a really terrible piece of writing. It is a melancholy truth that—as Harvey Shapiro's smart new anthology, *Poets of World War II,* reminds us—both the best war poems and the best anti-war poems generally come from the ranks of the soldiers who do the fighting and the reporters who cover them. That said, it is noteworthy and bears repetition that at a time of intense crisis and color-coded alerts, so many of us turn instinctively to poetry not only for inspiration and consolation but as a form of action and for a sense of community.

Poets and poetry couldn't stay out of the news last year. A poet was nominated and confirmed as the new chairman of the National Endowment for the Arts: the choice of Dana Gioia garnered rare acclaim on all fronts at a divisive time. "This is a moment of marvelous possibility,"

Gioia told a New Hampshire gathering of state poets shortly after assuming his new post. "You poets laureate may be working on little or no budget, with few or no resources. What you have at your disposal may be merely symbolic. But we poets are masters of using symbols." Gioia launched a major Shakespeare initiative that will subsidize productions of the Bard's works nationwide. The Pentagon chipped in some extra cash to extend the tour to include military bases. Gioia also disclosed plans for a Shakespeare recitation contest, which he hopes will lead to a national competition encouraging the memorization of great poems. The career of a serious poet is evidently not inconsistent with the administrative and strategic demands of running an important government agency or, for that matter, a treasured cultural foundation. Edward Hirsch, whose poem "The Desire Manuscripts" was selected by Yusef Komunyakaa for this year's anthology, took over the presidency of the Guggenheim Foundation in January 2003. At a poetry forum at the New School University, Hirsch was asked to name a formative experience in his becoming a poet. Like others asked this question, Hirsch replied by naming an unsung heroine, in his case Professor Carol Parsons at Grinnell College, who "taught me in my freshman year that poetry is an art of making, and not just of self-expression."

"I am all for poets invading all walks of American life," Billy Collins declared, and the invasion shows no signs of letting up. The world of high stakes poker is the latest field to be conquered. James McManus, whose work appeared in the 1991 (Strand) and 1994 (Ammons) volumes in this series, made more than a quarter million dollars playing championship poker a few years ago. McManus commented on "poker lit" and added significantly to it with his new book *Positively Fifth Street.* It speaks to the enhanced celebrity of the poet in American society that you can collect "poet cards" featuring portraits of Donald Hall, Carolyn Kizer, Adrienne Rich, and worthy others (Mille Grazie Press, Santa Barbara, California) or that Tebot Bach, a nonprofit organization in Huntington, California, is producing a Southern California poets swimsuit calendar with Carol Muske-Dukes, David St. John, Charles Harper Webb, and Suzanne Lummis among the pinups: "You've admired their words, now marvel at the sheer beauty of their bodies!"

Christmas came early to *Poetry* magazine with the November 2002 announcement that Ruth Lilly, the heiress of the Lilly pharmaceutical fortune, had left more than $100 million—by some estimates close to $150 million—to the Chicago-based monthly that Harriet Monroe founded in 1912. It was the single biggest bequest ever given to a poetry organization. As a young woman many years ago, Lilly had submitted her poems to the magazine, but the editors had never accepted any, a fact that spurred wags to quip that rejecting her was the best thing *Poetry* ever did—well, maybe second best after publishing "The Love Song of J. Alfred Prufrock" back in 1915. Proving that poetry—the work itself rather than all the stuff around it—is the news that stays new, T. S. Eliot's great poem continues to cast its spell on English majors and creative people across the arts. A television series (*Push, Nevada*) featuring an IRS agent named Prufrock wowed the critics last year, while director Michael Petroni's new movie with Guy Pearce and Helena Bonham Carter derives not only its title (*Till Human Voices Wake Us*) but its imagery (water) and action (a drowning) from the conclusion of "Prufrock," which the movie quotes reverently. Another allusion to Eliot's poem occurs in a recent episode of *Law and Order*. "I have measured out my life with coffee spoons," a perjurous defense attorney says. "For once in my life I dared to eat the peach," he adds, peach in this context serving as shorthand for a sexual tryst with a homicidal femme fatale. Not to be outdone in the homage-to-Eliot sweepstakes, HBO's hit series *Six Feet Under* gives us an amorous couple in bed sharing poetry. The man says the original title of the poem is "He Do the Police in Different Voices," and the woman says she likes that title more than the one the poet settled on: "The Waste Land."

In an age that looks at ostentatious controversy as the next best thing after celebrity, some poets avoid controversy, some court it, and some have it thrust upon them. The newly appointed poet laureate of Canada created a stir when he denounced "slam" poetry as "crude" and "revolting." The poet laureate of California resigned after admitting he had falsified his résumé. Justice J. Michael Eakin of the Pennsylvania Supreme Court, nicknamed the "poetic justice of Pennsylvania," was rebuked for writing a dissenting opinion in seven quatrains and a footnote. The case hinged on whether a lie about the value of an engagement ring invalidated a prenuptial agreement. ("He has also," the *New York Times*'s Adam Liptak, reported, "ruled in rhyme in cases involving animals and car repair companies.") Nothing will stop a book columnist from building a piece on the demonstrably false premise that only poets read poetry and therefore the poets might as well make themselves useful in other ways. At the same time, *poetry* remains the journalist's honorific of choice when the subject is rock'n'roll, political oratory, the grace of Kobe Bryant driving to the basket, or almost anything other than poetry itself. "Like every muscle car before it, SUVs are big, dangerous and superfluous, but they're also poetry made of metal," writes the *Wall Street Journal*'s David Brooks.

Vaclav Havel stepped down as president of the Czech Republic, but the tradition of the poet as international diplomat continues. Dominique de Villepin, the French foreign minister who fenced with Colin Powell at the U. N. Security Council last February, is working on a poetry manuscript. In at least one respect, he is like his American counterparts. Asked to recite a poem, he obliges by reading three. In what almost sounds like a paraphrase of an early poem by the late Kenneth Koch ("You Were Wearing"), the young fashion designer Behnaz Sarafpour tells of wanting her fall line to reflect the poetry she is reading: there is an Emily Dickinson suit ("about hope"), a Herman Melville long blue dress ("about creation of art"), and a couple of Lord Byron dresses with poems embroidered on the hems. A perhaps more unexpected lover of verse is William J. Lennox, Jr., the superintendent in charge of the military academy at West Point, a three-star general who earned a doctorate in English from Princeton with a dissertation on American war poets. Speaking to a reporter, the general made a point of stressing the educative importance of a poem of bitter disillusionment, such as Wilfred Owen's "Dulce et Decorum Est," written from the Western Front in World War I. "Most cadets romanticize war," he said. "They need these images from war to help them understand. Confronting this romanticism is what education is about."

Yusef Komunyakaa, who has made unforgettable poetry out of his experiences in Vietnam, has brought to the editing of this volume—the seventeenth in the *Best American Poetry* series—an acute sensitivity to the moral temper of the times and a strong attraction to works of seriousness and ambition. He has written that he chose to write poetry "because of the conciseness, the precision, the imagery, and the music in the lines," qualities that he prizes in the works of others. "I like the idea that the meaning of my poetry is not always on the surface and that people may return to the work," he says. "Sometimes I may not like a poem in the first reading, but, when I go back and read it again, there is a growth that has happened within me, and I become a participant rather than just a reader." We hope the poems gathered here reward multiple readings and hasten a similar transformation of the reader into a sort of participant by proxy. Nor are the subjects limited to "World History," "Jihad," and "After Your Death," to cite three titles. There are poems on blues and jazz (a Komunyakaa enthusiasm I share), poems of wit and invention, a prose poem honoring Max Jacob and a verse poem "After Horace." There are poems in unusual forms, poems on themes ranging from film noir and the conventions of the murder mystery to bread, asparagus, and the restaurant business, as well as poems that take big, important concepts—"Beauty," "Success," "The Music of Time," "A History of Color"—and render them in compelling terms and true. Many names familiar to followers of contemporary poetry are here, but it is the newcomers that may most excite the book's editors and readers. In *The Best American Poetry 2003* two poets are represented with their first published poems: George Higgins (born 1956) and Heather Moss (born 1973). One reason this pleases me especially is that it shows there is a democracy at work even during the very nonegalitarian processes of exercising judgments and making critical discriminations. The oldest poet in this year's edition is Ruth Stone (born 1915, and still going strong, coming off a year when she won the National Book Award). The youngest is Anna Ziegler (born 1979, and thus nine years old when this series commenced). Poems were selected from more than forty magazines; many more were consulted and read with pleasure. Every year of working on this series has renewed my appreciation of the work that magazine editors do, usually without much fanfare but with extraordinary generosity of spirit.

In 2003 occurred the centenary of an event that happened almost invisibly at the Statue of Liberty: the presentation of a bronze plaque with Emma Lazarus's immortal words on it to the War Department post commander on Bedloe's Island in May 1903. Lazarus had written her sonnet "The New Colossus" for a fund-raising auction in 1883. It was not recited, nor was Lazarus present, at the ceremony dedicating the Bartholdi statue in New York harbor. Largely forgotten, the poem went unmentioned in the obituaries when Lazarus died a year later, in 1887. At the time people thought of the woman with the torch in her hand as a monument to fraternal Franco-American relations going back to George Washington and the Marquis de Lafayette. The statue honored liberty, the glow of enlightenment, but the full significance of the site and the statue was not realized until Emma Lazarus's lines were engraved in the public memory, and that did not happen overnight, for poetry can take a long time to achieve its full effect. The plaque hung obscurely on an interior wall of the statue's pedestal from 1903 until a popular effort in the 1930s succeeded in making that great symbol synonymous with the "Mother of Exiles," a welcoming refuge for "the wretched refuse" of Europe. The statue in the harbor was there, a lovely sight, but it remained for a poet to articulate its true significance: "Give me your tired, your poor, / Your huddled masses yearning to breathe free." For many of us who fondly recall climbing the stairs of the Statue with a beloved parent or with a busload of grade school chums, the famous peroration is so familiar that we may be blinded from noticing its literary excellence. But "The New Colossus" is not as familiar as it once was, and it deserves close study, perhaps in conjunction with another great sonnet occasioned by statuary, such as Shelley's "Ozymandias." At a moment of global anxiety it is good to consider this vital part of the American Dream as Emma Lazarus expressed it in a poem that made something happen— something as nearly sublime as the promise of liberty and a fair shake to people who had known only despotism and terror and danger and despair.

Yusef Komunyakaa was born in Bogalusa, Louisiana, in 1947. After graduating from Bogalusa's Central High School in 1965, he enlisted in the United States Army and was sent to Vietnam, where he served as a correspondent for (and later editor of) the military newspaper, *The Southern Cross*. Educated at the University of Colorado, Colorado State University, and the University of California at Irvine, he is the author of *Pleasure Dome: New and Collected Poems, 1975–1999* (Wesleyan University Press, 2001), *Talking Dirty to the Gods* (Farrar, Straus, and Giroux, 2000), and *Thieves of Paradise* (Wesleyan, 1998). For *Neon Vernacular: New and Selected Poems, 1977–1989* he received both the Pulitzer Prize and the Kingsley Tufts Poetry Award. His prose is collected in *Blue Notes: Essays, Interviews, and Commentaries,* which appeared in the University of Michigan Press's Poets on Poetry Series in 2000. In collaboration with Sascha Feinstein, he edited *The Jazz Poetry Anthology* (1991). He has taught at Princeton University, Indiana University, and Washington University in St. Louis.

INTRODUCTION

Yusef Komunyakaa

◇　◇　◇

In John Hawkes's novel *Travesty,* the narrator speaks to his daughter's lover as he drives the three of them toward death:

> "Murder, Henri? Well, that is precisely the trouble with you poets. In your pessimism you ape the articulation you achieve in written words, you are able to recite your poems as an actor his lines, you consider yourselves quite exempt from all those rules of behavior that constrict us lesser-privileged men in feet, hands, loins, mouths. Yet in the last extremity you cry moral wolf. . . ."

With an almost incantatory irony, "lesser-privileged" ricochets in the brain; it echoes a question that has dogged me for years: Are some American poets writing from a privileged position—especially after the fiery 1960s and '70s—from a place that reflects the illusions of class through language and aesthetics, and is the "new" avant-garde an old aspect of the high-brow and low-brow divide within the national psyche? And there's also this terrifying thought: Are there poets who have purposefully set out to create work that (doesn't matter) only matters to the anointed, those who might view themselves as privileged above content? I know such questions were on my mind as I read numerous periodicals, searching for poems that touched me through content and aesthetics. It has been rewarding to work with David Lehman on *The Best American Poetry 2003.* For those who have hammered nails into poetry's coffin again and again, as if afflicted with wishful thinking, I was delighted to be reminded that American poetry is in steady hands. Though this anthology is limited to seventy-five poems, I still wish all the deserving voices could have been included.

Also, while reading the healthy heap of literary magazines, I was reminded that there exists a poetry that borders on cultivated solecism and begs theorists to decipher it. But it isn't for me to say if this so-called exploratory movement verges on a literary deception, though it does follow an era that praised content and the empirical.

Yes, sometimes our artists and intellectuals let us down through silence and erasure. This was provocatively driven home to me in Lewis M. Dabney's introduction to Edmund Wilson's *The Sixties:*

> The public world is here only a backdrop for Wilson's account of his own experience. The assassination of Kennedy receives a single biting paragraph. Wilson supports Johnson till the escalation of the Vietnam War, which occasions an argument with a summer friend in Talcottville that—characteristic of the times—almost comes to blows. He is pleased, in 1966, when Robert Kennedy is reported to be reading one of his books while waiting at the polls in New York. The next year [Robert] Lowell tells him of the protest march on the Pentagon, but by now his energies are given to the expanded *Dead Sea Scrolls.* He notes a fraying in the American social fabric, from upstate to the changing appearance of New York City. In 1968, however, the journal leaves unmentioned Johnson's decision not to run for reelection, the assassination of Robert Kennedy and Martin Luther King, Jr., the uproar at the Democratic convention.

We know that many of our artists and intellectuals didn't suffer such amnesia; however, some did. Can we risk a deficit in memory, in the erasure of recent history? Where Wilson's head seems to have been momentarily filled with a certain kind of forgetting, his friend Robert Lowell writes one of his most poignant poems during the 1960s that cannot be dismissed or easily forgotten, as is shown in these first six stanzas of "For the Union Dead":

> The old South Boston Aquarium stands
> in a Sahara of snow now. Its broken windows are boarded.
> The bronze weathervane cod has lost half its scales.
> The airy tanks are dry.
>
> Once my nose crawled like a snail on the glass;
> my hand tingled
> to burst the bubbles
> drifting from the noses of the cowed, compliant fish.

My hand draws back. I often sigh still
for the dark downward and vegetating kingdom
of the fish and reptile. One morning last March,
I pressed against the new barbed and galvanized

fence on the Boston Common. Behind their cage,
yellow dinosaur steam shovels were grunting
as they cropped up tons of mush and grass
to gouge their underworld garage.

Parking lots luxuriate like civic
sand piles in the heart of Boston.
A girdle of orange, Puritan-pumpkin-colored girders
braces the tingling Statehouse, shaking

over the excavations, as it faces Colonel Shaw
and his bell-cheeked Negro infantry
on St. Gaudens' shaking Civil War relief,
propped by a plank splint against the garage's earthquake.

With lines drawn in the dirt—intellectual and moral, social and aesthetic, cultural and political—a poem such as "For the Union Dead" could waylay friendships and allegiances. Robert Lowell wrote his poem in the middle of the Civil Rights movement. Of course, he wasn't the only American poet to respond to "the sixties" with verve and fervor as Carolyn Forché's important 1993 anthology, *Against Forgetting: Twentieth-Century Poetry of Witness,* attests to with astounding examples. I cannot forget that some critics and poets spoke disparagingly about *Against Forgetting.* In fact, the title underlines what many Americans were trying to do, especially in regard to the 1960s and '70s; they were lamenting the fall of the good old days with good old boys at the moral helm, and were talking about the newly frayed fabric of American society. The reverberation of Allen Ginsberg's *Howl* was still in the sacred air of possibility. Some artists seem to desire a reinvestment in silence; the phrase "silent majority" echoed. The 1950s were peering around the corner again. Apathy again had us in a stranglehold; *reverse discrimination* became a mantra. And some poets began to pen their own unique silence through a language that deliberately confuses and blurs meaning. Poems began to sound like coded messages to the void, maps to nowhere, as if language shouldn't *mean*—an anti-poetry. In his book, *Consilience,* Edward O. Wilson says:

> The defining quality of the arts is the expression of the human condition by mood and feeling, calling into play all the senses, evoking both order and disorder.

In some of the exploratory texts, those of *over*-experimentation, disorder becomes the norm—a blurred design that is supposed to depict wit, opacity, and difficulty as virtue. And Wilson continues, saying:

> Artistic inspiration common to everyone in varying degree rises from the artesian wells of human nature. Its creations are meant to be delivered directly to the sensibilities of the beholder without analytic explanation. Creativity is therefore humanistic in the fullest sense. Works of enduring value are those truest to these origins. It follows that even the greatest works of art might be understood fundamentally with knowledge of the biologically evolved epigenetic rules that guided them.

Content over aesthetics is problematic also; there has to exist a synthesis, one informing the other. In the middle of the Civil Rights movement, in 1966, at the Black Writers' Conference at Fisk University, four years after Robert Hayden published *A Ballad of Remembrance* in which poems such as "Homage to the Empress of the Blues," "Middle Passage," "Runagate Runagate," appeared, he was chastised because of the attention he'd given to the aesthetic character of his poetry. One has only to hear the language of the first stanza in the title poem, "A Ballad of Remembrance," to see where his critics went wrong:

> Quadroon mermaids, Afro angels, black saints
> balanced upon the switchblades of that air
> and sang. Tight streets unfolding to the eye
> like fans of corrosion and elegiac lace
> crackled with their singing: Shadow of time. Shadow of blood.

Of course, this is a cogent example of form shaped by content. Poetry encourages us to have dialogue through the observed, the felt, and the imaginary, in this world and beyond, and few seem to have known this better than Robert Hayden, W. H. Auden's faithful student. His acknowledgment to craft and voice is clearly illustrated in the poem's penultimate stanza:

Then you arrived, meditative, ironic,
richly human; and your presence was shore where I rested
released from the hoodoo of that dance, where I spoke
with my true voice again.

Gwendolyn Brooks was also "dissed" at the Fisk conference. But where she gave in, Hayden stood his ground—troubled within.

Oftentimes, the poetry of erasure presents a false dazzle that lays on white space—indifferent—and seems to emulate an epicurean netherworld that's contrary to Edward O. Wilson's thoughts on the artist. Indeed, this need to belittle and mistrust content, at times, seems like a kind of high-brow slapstick that takes us away from the body, making us even more indebted to insignificance and abstraction. This makes one think of William Carlos Williams's observations about language:

> There are plenty who use the language well, fully as well as Pound, but for trivial purposes, either journalism, fiction or even verse. I mean the usual stroking of the material without penetration where anything of momentous significance is instinctively avoided. There are on the other hand poets of considerable seriousness who simply do not know what language is and unconsciously load their compositions with minute anachronisms as many as dead hairs on a mangy dog.

I believe content is a part of process, which is essential to technique and form. There isn't any topic that's taboo; however, there has to exist refined principles of aesthetics. This folly by the so-called new avant-garde, those exploratory poets, seems like an attempt to undermine the importance of recent history, to introduce tonal and linguistic flux as the center of the poem—anything goes because the poet or the poem's speaker doesn't exist. It's death in language. At times, it seems that this movement embraces our obsession with technology. The scrambled, amorphous texture of most exploratory poetry also parallels what happened in modern jazz after John Coltrane died in 1967, whenever a musician attempted to get away from the blues, from melody. David G. Such says in *Avant-Garde Jazz Musicians:*

> Most of the criticisms leveled against out jazz generally focus on features in the music that are "cacophonous" and too difficult for average listeners to comprehend. Out jazz, with its rapidly played flurries of tones, squeaks and squawks, collective improvisation,

variable rhythms, and so forth, aggressively challenges most listeners' expectations and can burden them with too many complex bits of information.

I believe it was Miles Davis who said, "The reason I stopped playing ballads is because I love them so much." Afraid of tonal narrative, the story the music could tell? Afraid of being uncool and growing old, or duped by the sexual bluster of rock 'n' roll? Plus, some jazz musicians were still jamming in after-hour sets for a few drinks on the house and sheer joy of playing together, hardly making ends meet. But how could Miles have recorded *Sketches of Spain* and *The Birth of the Cool,* and then betray himself playing on fusion pieces? Likewise, for the poet who has always embraced content as form, any experimentation not in service of meaning is anti-poetry. After the movement era—as well as during—there's an effort to diminish the importance of the 1960s and '70s, to roll back the clocks. It is interesting to consider this: when voices that were based on experience began to rise from the fringes of our society, the new avant-garde, armored with critical theory, began to make "preemptive strikes" at those who saw content as a reflection of their lives and visions. The witness became suspect—seen as passé, old-timey, unevolved, and not part of a progressive outlook. Afraid of any accusation of sentimentality, for some poets distance and detachment developed. Often, if the poet gives the speaker in a poem feelings, he or she risks being called retrograde and boring.

One question that dogs the poet is this: Where is poetry going? Isn't it our duty to keep it exciting? Recently, we have invested a lot of energy in the spoken word movement. *Def Poetry Jam on Broadway* is playing at the moment, and some people are walking away, saying, "Very little of it works on the page." Poetry and music? Well, the idea of the lyre takes us to the lyric poem, doesn't it? When there's mutual respect between musician and poet, some provocative collaborations can take place—sometimes without the poet's say-so. Here's what I found on my CD shelves, some examples not that recent: Genny Lim/Francis Wong's *Devotee,* with Glenn Horiuchi and Elliot Humberto Kavee; Yevgeny Yevtushenko/Dmitri Shostakovich's *Babi Yar,* with Men of the New York Choral Artists and the New York Philharmonic; Philip Glass/Allen Ginsberg's *Hydrogen Jukebox*; Elliot Goldenthal's *Fire Water Paper: A Vietnam Oratorio,* with Yo-Yo Ma, Ann Panagulias, James Maddalena, Ngan-Khoi Vietnamese Children's Chorus, and Pacific Symphony Orchestra conducted by Carl St. Clair; Langston Hughes/Charles Mingus's *Weary Blues,* with Leonard Feathers. I couldn't find Marion Brown's recording of Jean Toomer's prose poem *Karintha.* However, I did find Branford Marsalis's *Scenes in the City,* with narrator Wendell Pierce speaking a rendition of this Mingus piece (not really poetry, though Mingus says he was influenced as an artist by a "streetcorner poet in L.A."). What really caught my attention are a couple sentences in A. B. Spellman's notes: ". . . We are in an eclectic age, when there aren't a lot of brilliant new ideas around. The avant-garde of the 1960s left a lot of innovation to be resolved, and that's what a mainstream does." Indeed, maybe that's the problem with some of the exploratory poets, where the text of a poem may seem muddled through *over*-experimentation: In this quest for a few brilliant new ideas, with the Ego riding shotgun, to what extent can language be distorted before it loses meaning, before it erases itself?

Keeping the idea of erasure in the foreground, one of my favorite spoken-word compositions is "Sing Me a Song of Songmy," cut in 1971. I think that this tantalizing LP was clearly ahead of its time; and it's like a well-kept secret. *Sing Me a Song of Songmy,* subtitled "A fantasy for electromagnetic tape," features Freddie Hubbard and his quintet, with reciters, chorus, string orchestra, Hammond organ, synthesized and processed sounds, composed and realized by Ilhan Mimaroglu. Here's an example of the poetry: Nha-Khe's "Lullaby for a Child in War"; Fazil Husnu Daglarca's "Poverty," "Colored Soldier," and "Before the Bombs Struck the Dark Breasts." And there are also haunting quotations from Søren Kierkegaard's essay "The Individual." The entire CD emphasizes content as well as form and structure—if content forces one to think about all wars, not merely the war in Vietnam. I think of Muriel Rukeyser's statement in "The Life of Poetry":

> We are a people tending toward democracy at the level of hope; on another level, the economy of the nation, the empire of business within the republic, both include in their basic premise the concept of perpetual warfare. It is the history of the idea of war that is beneath our other histories.

With September 11 still resounding, we sought poetry that embodies content.

Why poetry? Well, it seems the natural direction, a way to calm our fears and anger. Whether attempting to see into the mystery of things or the human soul, poetry has long been the instrument and the path.

Some of our most sacred texts are composed in "poetic" language, and this is Edward O. Wilson's point when he says:

> Recognize that when introits and invocations prickle the skin we are in the presence of poetry, and the soul of the tribe, something that will outlive the particularities of sectarian belief, and perhaps belief in God itself.

Wilson is speaking of a people's tongue and the power of language—perhaps even prior to our naming of things—a "poetry" that helps us to see into the flux, spiritually and psychologically, because it assists us in facing the immensity of primordial mystery. I'm not suggesting here that our first utterance was a prayer. In thinking about September 11 and poetry, it is important to underline the poems we sought, to think about why we embraced them. Why W. H. Auden's "September 1, 1939" or Marianne Moore's "What Are Years?"; why Edwin Arlington Robinson, Carlos Drummond de Andrade, Czeslaw Milosz, and the other voices? Maybe it has almost everything to do with content and aesthetics, with language as communication.

And now (February 2003) there's war talk. We have a long roster of voices that have spoken against human violence: even those poems that are directly about war, made of blood and guts, are in fact anti-war—from translations of Homer to the poetry on Desert Storm, Bosnia, and Somalia. But few have erasure at their nexus. So, in this light, it is more than interesting to consider the following invitation: *Laura Bush requests the pleasure of your company at a reception and White House Symposium on "Poetry and the American Voice" on Wednesday, February 12, 2003, at one o'clock   East Entrance   The White House Salute to America's Authors Series.* Let me say this from the onset: I do think that Ms. Bush's gesture is right, but the timing completely wrong. There's hawkish talk about war in the White House, and this is contrary to the numerous American poets who patterned their hearts and visions on Walt Whitman: "I rose from the chill ground and folded my soldier well in his blanket, / And buried him where he fell." Of course, as you probably already know by now, the White House event was canceled after Sam Hamill sent out his invitation:

> "War looms on the horizon. I live in a navy town and worked for the navy for nearly 40 years, but I believe that this is the wrong war at the wrong time. I don't expect anyone else to agree with me, but if you do, send a poem for peace to Sam."

Almost overnight, Sam received over five thousand poems. And on February 17 at Lincoln Center's Avery Fisher Hall, The Not in Our Name Statement of Conscience presented *Poems Not Fit for the White House*. I don't think that a single poet from the exploratory movement read that night to a packed hall of people who trudged through snow to hear poetry.

Recently, I lost two very dear people in my life. Both loved wearing fantastic hats made of beads and satin, felt and feathers, some almost somber and others bright as a peacock at daybreak.

My paternal grandmother, Mrs. Elsie Magee Otis, was a churchgoing woman, born in 1906 and raised in a small black village, and she was known to say, "Honey, you can't believe the changes I seen in my lifetime." Outside of Hackley, Louisiana, in Franklinton, *Magee* is stenciled across public buildings. But these are the white Magees; lately, however, the older white ones have been saying to the black ones: "Damnit, we are family." Yes, indeed, my grandmother saw changes. She spent the last few years of her long life at the Rest Haven Nursing Home in Bogalusa, Louisiana. Sometimes, she'd just start singing her favorite spiritual, "You Got to Move," and doctors, nurses, the staff, and visitors, everyone would crowd around her. The language in the song, what W. E. B. Du Bois called "sorrow songs," seemed to momentarily empower her. The song was always strong, but her voice grew feeble whenever she'd stop singing. At her funeral in a small country church, one of her close friends, Mrs. Verlean Bickham (the Bickhams are also kin to the Magees) sang "You Got to Move":

> You maybe rich
> You maybe poor
> But when the Lord calls
> You got to move
>
> You maybe high
> You maybe low
> But when the Lord calls
> You got to move

The song continues for a few more verses. But there's something about this piece that possesses the power and presence of folk poetry. It has content.

For the past five years, Zoe Anglesey was my close friend and confidante. Usually, she knew where and how to contact me, whether in Florence, New Orleans, or only God knows where. By contrast, her memorial service was held at the Lafayette Avenue Presbyterian Church, 85 South Oxford Street, in Brooklyn, the same block she'd lived on for years. This is the church where Frederick Douglass once spoke. The historic stained-glass windows rise and loom—thirteen of which were created by Louis Tiffany himself. There's also the "Miracle of Creation" window in the Lecture Room, a part of three panels, one of which is on display at the Metropolitan Museum of Art. And we can't forget that Marianne Moore's poem "The Steeple Jack" describes the removal of the church's steeple. These days the church is also home to the arts: The Audre Lorde Project, BAM 651 Arts, The InterSchool Orchestras of New York, Uptown String Quartet, and so forth. It was the perfect place to remember an activist poet and intellectual who cared about content in the arts. One of the most telling moments came when the poet Carl Hancock Rux read a letter that Zoe e-mailed to him on March 15, 2001. Here's an excerpt from Zoe's letter:

> Languages are disappearing along with the peoples who speak them, and they represent the ancient sources of our cultures. The movements to preserve and conserve the green of the earth— we are already buying water. Rich folks have the beautiful spots of the earth bought up and the remaining forests will soon be deserts. What future do we have for our young ones? Many people in Africa and South America are facing deserts that once were green and productive when war, exploitation and over-population set forces in motion to speed up the whole process of the extinction of the people on the land and the land going to desert. Movement? We just saw a coup. Our right to vote was scorned by the highest court in the land. Two governors conspired to rob the election. What is the penalty?
>
> There is no movement to prevent this. Instead sex scandals wag in the faces of those who were articulate on behalf of a passive population. Movement? When many of my college students admit to watching t.v. 3 to 7 hours a day—that's a half day's or whole day's work. We NEED a movement to empower people with the spirit of life and that spirit depends on working for one's life, family and community. Work gives us the connections to others and provides the ligaments to strong group action when it is required. Our val-

ues are at stake. The major poets live and die. Poets are the ones, as Neruda knew, who can articulate what ordinary people cannot or are too timid to articulate. This is part but not all of the poet's calling. As you mentioned, Carl, craft, letting the art develop, learning the craft, and letting the art exist for itself too—the freedom to create art—even that is under threat with this NYC Mayor and U.S. President. It's up to us, just like a day's work, to keep on keepin' on—on all fronts, on all issues.

These two women whom I lost from my life had more than hats in common: both were seers, too. One was unlettered, and the other was just downright gifted and caring as a poet and a citizen. The two of them would have known exactly what Martin Luther King, Jr., meant in his "I Have a Dream" speech when he says, "I have a dream my four little children will one day live in a nation where they will not be judged by the color of their skin but by the *content* [my italics] of their character."

Not that we strive or wish to become Borges's infamous character who cannot forget a single sensation, who's imprisoned in his skin and brain, unable to venture toward the future. But as poets, as artists, we do want meaning to remain in our words, and not have the essence of our lives and visions become like that moment when Robert Rauschenberg erases the de Kooning drawing and says that the erasure is his work of art.

The End of Out of the Past

(RKO, 1947)

◊ ◊ ◊

"I never told you I was anything but what I am," she says.
Black and white, the sunset behind Lake Tahoe looks spectacular.
She turns and goes upstairs, his chance to light a cigarette
and dial the operator. She slips a pistol into her briefcase,
gives the bedroom a cursory final glance. A moment later,
sitting on the couch, he hands her a shot of brandy.
"Thanks," she says. *"Por nada,"* he answers, pouring one
for himself. She says she thinks they both deserve a break. "We deserve
each other," he replies, and wings his glass into the empty fireplace.
She's unperturbed, strictly business, already in Mexico.
His sleepy expression shows he knows exactly where they're going.
Night has already covered most of the country. The airwaves
are vibrating with the strains of "Sentimental Journey," "Satin Doll,"
and "String of Pearls." As they get into his Chevy stationwagon,
I could be five and just waking up from another nightmare.
Half the world is lying in ruins.

from *London Review of Books*

from *A Locked Room*

◇　◇　◇

> *"It must be assumed that somebody is telling
> the truth—else there is no legitimate mystery,
> and, in fact, no story at all."*
> —John Dickson Carr, *The Three Coffins*

1.

Traps are underfoot on every path. He who set them is bound
to property, waits to see if jaws glinting in moonlight will leave traces
when they close. He passes three doors on his way to find songs of grief

with interchangeable words and will go back over his steps past them
until negligence finds another place to keep its keys. I listen—no sound—
see three chairs, one outside each door. Even so, the hall does not invite delay
Another gas lamp flutters against the gravel path, reflected in steel teeth

so that pieces of light are cut out. Evidently he has left and not given
us the means to suspect him, but there is no ladder; how did he descend?
We need not risk crossing open sky if imagination alone will suffice.

4.

The registrar's narrative finds him across from her while voices crash
and drop onto the quilt, undamaged. He lives like a wolf, with the hunter's
　　　eye
upon him, in an apartment surrounded by cement that keeps knowledge
　　　interned.

Held fast, in secret, it squints and grows by sifting through mattress guts.
A steward offered vast sums of money that were refused and his eyeglasses
fell from the bridge of his nose before imagination could recover them. I
gently imply that madness will pass from belief through theory to the silent
     cavern

containing all that is not held true. He expresses no surprise at the scratched
     but
whole chicken bones littering the ground where dogs guard the entryway
for we both know they will choke if they break through to marrow.

5.

On the window ledge a vine is crushed as if by the weight of a person
preparing to jump. But just three feet separate the mulch-covered ground
from the sill, and any leap would involve, then, a desire to live.

The absence of trust is a turning point in our sense of what should happen
to the words *I saw a man.* The strange dissociation of matter has become
a balloon inflated with helium, floating over footsteps sinking profoundly
as they progress toward betrayal. Ankles and cobblestones don't mix

so all claims ably resist corroboration. I prepare again to enter the garden
under the pretense of looking for traces he might have left. But once inside
I will in fact rely on dreams to unveil both guilt and happiness.

9.

We ate breakfast together in the sunlit room. Her soft voice denied any
involvement, but I knew I'd never comfortably sign any statement sporting
her word. Like the steps of blistering blocked shoes on dedicated toes,

her syntax returned to the point in every sentence, wore down one section
of sound-damped floorboards at a pace intended to clash with scenery.
Our words foliate these walls but eventually erode their own means of
support. Behind them, my goals hide even from me although we share

an office, nap nodding together in the afternoons. But danger beckons
and though I confess with some shame that I fear the blinking lights atop
each skyline tower, in order to save birds of prey I will overcome myself.

10.

Now who remains in the room with me? With that question I lost control of all
I'd thought secure. Clad in remnants of an echoing gallery, the lady in black
left her voice behind to protect those who would walk under leaning ladders.

We took chances but never were able to find ourselves at home, instead
kept crossing borders and becoming visible. He escaped the fall
in a most unusual way. He sprang atop a wire fence just after the attack
and used grudges to keep his balance across the roof, break the pattern,

skip lightly atop the trap without triggering its jaws. I must loop a thread
around my wrist and carry my identity tucked in my sleeve instead of on it,
move past witnesses to take my place, wanting to whisper in every ear but
        silent.

from *Poetry Project Newsletter*

Dedicated to the One I Love

◇   ◇   ◇

It's simply hopeless, isn't it? Even if you begin
by postulating the existence of some exotic place—
a village of divine origin, or diabolical perhaps—
maybe a city of sin, or hindrances such as torpor and lust
(those are the ones I like best), whole days spent in bed,
wearing silk pajamas, sipping cappuccino, daydreaming—
going backwards in time (you could visit Paris in the first
half of the century if you wish), gliding down bannisters
and into the ballrooms of the past where, by some odd chance,
you already know the steps to all the dances, you, Darling,
would still become a politician, some charismatic figure
issuing proclamations at every hour. And no matter what you say
or said, it would create the illusion of making sense, inspiring shock,
warning of imminent and supreme crisis without end—and all
at once we'd be back in the dark ages, and then the desert—
and you would decide to leave (don't you always?), slipping on
your coat and glasses, (alas) and rushing off before the part begins
with Jacob wrestling the angels, and all the patriarchs go limp—

but you wouldn't resist gazing back (would you? just once?)
through the promised lens—to see me again, there where I am
forever lazing in bed, combing my long black hair over my shoulders
and nude breasts? Outside the sky is shimmering, and it's dusk
in Jerusalem (or is it Valencia or Madrid?), and someone is ringing
the doorbell again and again, and I am imagining God is as happy
with the world (unredeemed as it is) as an ant atop a wet, bruised
    peach.

from *Gargoyle*

27

Some Further Words

◊   ◊   ◊

Let me be plain with you, dear reader.
I am an old-fashioned man. I like
the world of nature despite its mortal
dangers. I like the domestic world
of humans, so long as it pays its debts
to the natural world, and keeps its bounds.
I like the promise of Heaven. My purpose
is a language that can repay just thanks
and honor for those gifts, a tongue
set free from fashionable lies.

Neither this world nor any of its places
is an "environment." And a house
for sale is not a "home." Economics
is not "science," nor "information" knowledge.
A knave with a degree is a knave. A fool
in a public office is not a "leader."
A rich thief is a thief. And the ghost
of Arthur Moore, who taught me Chaucer,
returns in the night to say again:
"Let me tell you something, boy.
An intellectual whore is a whore."

The world is babbled to pieces after
the divorce of things from their names.
Ceaseless preparation for war
is not peace. Health is not procured
by sale of medication, or purity
by the addition of poison. Science

at the bidding of the corporations
is knowledge reduced to merchandise;
it is a whoredom of the mind,
and so is the art that calls this "progress."
So is the cowardice that calls it "inevitable."

I think the issues of "identity" mostly
are poppycock. We are what we have done,
which includes our promises, includes
our hopes, but promises first. I know
a "fetus" is a human child.
I loved my children from the time
they were conceived, having loved
their mother, who loved them
from the time they were conceived
and before. Who are we to say
the world did not begin in love?

I would like to die in love as I was born,
and as myself, of life impoverished, go
into the love all flesh begins
and ends in. I don't like machines,
which are neither mortal nor immortal,
though I am constrained to use them.
(Thus the age perfects its clench.)
Some day they will be gone, and that
will be a glad and a holy day.
I mean the dire machines that run
by burning the world's body and
its breath. When I see an airplane
fuming through the once-pure sky
or a vehicle of the outer space
with its little inner space
imitating a star at night, I say,
"Get out of there!" as I would speak
to a fox or a thief in the henhouse.
When I hear the stock market has fallen,
I say, "Long live gravity! Long live
stupidity, error, and greed in the palaces
of fantasy capitalism!" I think

an economy should be based on thrift,
on taking care of things, not on theft,
usury, seduction, waste, and ruin.

My purpose is a language that can make us whole,
though mortal, ignorant, and small.
The world is whole beyond human knowing.
The body's life is its own, untouched
by the little clockwork of explanation.
I approve of death, when it comes in time
to the old. I don't want to live
on mortal terms forever, or survive
an hour as a cooling stew of pieces
of other people. I don't believe that life
or knowledge can be given by machines.
The machine economy has set afire
the household of the human soul,
and all the creatures are burning within it.

"Intellectual property" names
the deed by which the mind is bought
and sold, the world enslaved. We
who do not own ourselves, being free,
own by theft what belongs to God,
to the living world, and equally
to us all. Or how can we own a part
of what we only can possess
entirely? Life is a gift we have
only by giving it back again.
Let us agree: "the laborer is worthy
of his hire," but he cannot own what he knows,
which must be freely told, or labor
dies with the laborer. The farmer
is worthy of the harvest made
in time, but he must leave the light
by which he planted, grew, and reaped,
the seed immortal in mortality,
freely to the time to come. The land
too he keeps by giving it up,

as the thinker receives and gives a thought,
as the singer sings in the common air.

I don't believe that "scientific genius"
in its naive assertions of power
is equal either to nature or
to human culture. Its thoughtless invasions
of the nuclei of atoms and cells
and this world's every habitation
have not brought us to the light
but sent us wandering farther through
the dark. Nor do I believe
"artistic genius" is the possession
of any artist. No one has made
the art by which one makes the works
of art. Each one who speaks speaks
as a convocation. We live as councils
of ghosts. It is not "human genius"
that makes us human, but an old love,
an old intelligence of the heart
we gather to us from the world,
from the creatures, from the angels
of inspiration, from the dead—
an intelligence merely nonexistent
to those who do not have it, but
to those who have it more dear than life.

And just as tenderly to be known
are the affections that make a woman and a man
their household and their homeland one.
These too, though known, cannot be told
to those who do not know them, and fewer
of us learn them, year by year.
These affections are leaving the world
like the colors of extinct birds,
like the songs of a dead language.

Think of the genius of the animals,
every one truly what it is:

gnat, fox, minnow, swallow, each made
of light and luminous within itself.
They know (better than we do) how
to live in the places where they live.
And so I would like to be a true
human being, dear reader—a choice
not altogether possible now.
But this is what I'm for, the side
I'm on. And this is what you should
expect of me, as I expect it of
myself, though for realization we
may wait a thousand or a million years.

May–August 2001

from *American Poetry Review*

Curse

◇ ◇ ◇

May breath for a dead moment cease as jerking your

head upward you hear as if in slow motion floor

collapse evenly upon floor as one hundred and ten

floors descend upon you.

May what you have made descend upon you.
May the listening ears of your victims   their eyes   their

breath

enter you, and eat like acid
the bubble of rectitude that allowed you breath.

May their breath now, in eternity, be your breath.

★

Now, as you wished, you cannot for us
not be. May this be your single profit.

Of your rectitude at last disenthralled, you
seek the dead. Each time you enter them

they spit you out. The dead find you are not food.

Out of the great secret of morals, *the imagination to enter the skin of another,* what I have made is a curse.

from *The Threepenny Review*

DIANN BLAKELY

Rambling on My Mind

DUET WITH ROBERT JOHNSON #33

◊ ◊ ◊

And now they've found your grave again, your grandson too,
His claim to the estate—T-shirts, CDs, movies

And postage stamps, their cigarettes airbrushed—

Ruled valid when he got himself a witness, his aunt,
Whose deathbed memory rambled to your origins,
    The pants and lovecalls rising from underbrush

After a fish fry, rising from a ditch right next to hers.
No one predicts the mess of truth's red afterbirth,

Not me, fumbling with *devilment* and forebears,

Who claims the first woman killed by Nat Turner's gang,
Two war suicides, a master who damned slaveholding
    And plunged his fortune past what the market bears,

Past—he prayed—*mean things. Mean things* like those you claimed for songs,
Which foretold more bad news: factory and stockyard closings,

King shot in Memphis, schoolkids selling crack

By fallen tractor sheds. All great migrations done,
And done for. *You treat me so unkind,* sing thousands gone
    Half-mad with hearts that history has cracked

Like a sun-warped guitar, ditched and almost forgotten—
My time ain't long, you sigh, edged near the door. What then

About that Greek guy who cut a ewe's throat

And watched ghosts bend to drink from its ditch-runnelled blood,
His rambling heart grown still? They rose in packs from Hades,
    Among them his own mother, her prophet's throat

A mess of wrinkles, to warn that her son's journey home
Would be long and kill all his men—he wept, his arms

Embracing loveless air three times. Truth sides

With history's open veins, we'll reprise when the curtain
Of that dimestore photo booth opens, its mirror stained
    And thumb-stamped by those called from the other side.

                    from *BOMB*

Art Tatum

◇   ◇   ◇

No stranger to the faith of eyes
asleep under the surgeon's lancet,
to time gambled with every try

that slit the foam of cataracts
where they pearled, he understood
the powers of sun to make us

loyal, what it is to shadow
twilight on the eye's horizon.
Then it came: the crumpling blow

that made desire final, the day
a neighbor blackjacked and robbed him,
flooding the blotter of his gaze.

And as the wounded eye welled up
with blindness, the other followed
blind: that night an ocular cup

of flashlight dwindled down the path
in his head, over pianos
as he saw them there, glazed in pitch.

Soon he grew into living proof
that darkness deepens the mind's ear.
It quickened what his hands were made of,

all those notes mapping the faces
of chords, touching the phantom shapes.
Finesse, yes, but not the mere lace

of fancy; more a conversation
among losses, each prick of light
dissolving in its constellation.

Once he sat by a radio,
listening to a dead friend, and played
along on the air piano.

As if his fingertips had eyes
gazing into music beneath
the music, dark, mute, buried alive.

from *The Paris Review*

from *1000 Lines*

◊   ◊   ◊

Ten notes. Two pentatonics. The blues scale
in the key of E: the City's secret
hymn sewn into cement knot work, sky work—
ten years, what can I remember of it?
Avenues, wind, salt-glazed estuary—
frieze panels; stone work of new-born blossoms,
tabernacles and cusped arches: brickwork
robed in saffron, Wednesday evening picnics,
asiago, fumé blanc in paper
cups. River talced with curatives of light:

ten years as chapters, scored and fluted, all
encrypted: the City's sky-box, soul-box—
the signs and omens: one Sunday, rookie
cops in training for suicide rescue
on the binderies of the Brooklyn Bridge:
their silhouettes, ideograms against
the river's vellum; one snowy Spring day,
two redtail hawks perched on a bare branch, one
holding a headless dove in its talon.
The end of love? Or a love offering?

Ten year hungers: a man eats raw chicken
out of the dumpster, while we eat raw fish
in the sushi bar; the lot swarming with
rats across from the gothic cathedral—
you can't figure out if you're depressed or
just unsatisfied—*and so what if my
mother wanted cornbread stuffing?*—baby

roaches in an ice cube at the diner;
reading a *New York Times* ad for silver
spoons, right next to a story on famine—

ten years: one hundred and twenty full moons,
give or take a few, underneath Amish
quilts made for us by Saloma Byler—
she would write: dear friend your quilt is ready—
(three years ago she died from breast cancer)—
wrapped in her double–wedding ring pattern,
we munched on low-fat Chubby Hubby, watched
screwball comedies: and the eight-second
TV parade replay of the police
striking a man fifty times with batons—

ten years: our bed: a desk, a couch, a horn,
a bird figurine, mortar and grinder,
a spoon for winnowing grains, a lemon
and palm branch in a bundle depicted,
a modern impression of ancient scales,
a boat without oars, where we heaved and hoed,
made mirth, shook in terror, sighed in relief,
fucked ten different ways, goose-down libation—
vowed to love God and walk in his footsteps—
ah, well . . . blade from a sickle, sickle blade—

ten red Fiestaware cups and saucers
I smashed on the kitchen floor: talk about
explosions. We fought every single day
for a year when we moved to the Village,
all stupid things really, it was clear, you
were not happy—your therapist said I
needed to get over my problems with
men, before we think about having kids—
my mother told me the day we married,
watch your temper. What temper? I asked her.

Tenebrionid: see darkling beetle,
from the Latin: one who avoids the light.
This isn't the movies, it's a marriage!

the real becomes visible not through close
attachments, but through close looking, atten-
tion, the mystic said, *is the soul's prayer.*
Remember your job interview—how I
bathed you—the rain forest trip—libations—
making love under Passover's full moon,
howler monkeys, Cieba trees, Mayan tombs—

tents packed we took a walk through the forest:
I imagined us just not going back,
we'd build a house in a tree that would last
us twenty rainy seasons, for nails we'd
use the spines of great big yellow flowers,
we would make our dollars from the green dye
in the leaves, our carpet a melody
of toucan feathers, each night we'd drain thick
resin into cups to share with our ghosts,
from cones we'd make a box spring (see below):

IOIOIOIOIOIOIOIOIO
IOIOIOIOIOIOIOIOIO
IOIOIOIOIOIOIOIOIO
IOIOIOIOIOIOIOIOIO
IOIOIOIOIOIOIOIOIO
IOIOIOIOIOIOIOIOIO
IOIOIOIOIOIOIOIOIO
IOIOIOIOIOIOIOIOIO
IOIOIOIOIOIOIOIOIO
IOIOIOIOIOIOIOIOIO

Ten summer trips back to San Antonio—
Saturday: Westside Mission Flea Market,
it's hard to see with a dust storm brewing:
the sky like a broth of childhood whippings—
objects speak, the soul just has to listen,
a woman tells us from a plywood tent
bathed in honey mesquite—the bargain's great!—
if you want cucumbers, there's a truck full,
and roosters, ten steel cages filled with—yes!—
roosters! snakes too! and one red cowboy boot—

ten bucks: a used world for sale, an antique
with just a piece of Panama missing,
a little KY will get it spinning—
you spot a nutcracker nude—oak nipples—
a vendor called the Rifleman, shoves a
pecan between her legs and gives a squeeze—
here's a ghost guitar, he says: and holds it
to the light, *needs no human touch to play*
three strums means death is calling, two a storm—
dust devils swirling: the smell of chili—

ten A.M.: the band is really cooking:
under the pavilion, a conjunto
accordion wails: *who were you thinking*
of when we were making love last night—red
wind, biker belts for babies, tripe tacos,
potent clouds everyone circle dancing—
an old rancher with a young man's body—
wasn't he just inside the rooster cage—
and the lean jeweled woman of seventy
he's dancing with?—*I think she was the snake*—

ten javelina hogs around the tent,
while I slept, you cooking a campfire
breakfast—remember that?—hiking the Lost
Gold Mine trail, ocotillo, cactus blooms,
pictographs of jaguar and prickly pear—
perfect margaritas at Ma Crosby's—
while hiking, I mimicked Charlie Chaplin
to make you laugh—we soaked in sulphur springs:
the desert moon five-by-five in the sky—
fat: as a pig raised on cherry milkshakes—

ten degrees past one hundred, ten past eight.
Stopping for breakfast in Presidio,
the heat capital of America,
and everyone at the Presidio
Cafe is having biscuits. Everyone
is having biscuits with Presidio
gravy. *These biscuits are good. These biscuits*

are good. Better than last week. Much better
than last week. Sure is hot today. It sure
is hot. Should we get some more? Huh? Should we?

Ten gifts you gave me that I've lost: a pair
of cut glass earrings; one of two crystal
Waterford candle holders; the lilac
Belle France dress for Passover, the year we
made matzo chili rellenos; several
pearl studs; a Starbucks travel mug (my last
present); the bottoms to my rodeo
pjs; The Collected Wallace Stevens;
a portable phone, and a black silk gown—
how could you lose a phone?—you used to say—

ten years shaped like a dog flute in combo
with a Jaracho harp; wrapped in the light
just before we hit the Hoover Dam. Or
wrapped in the white handkerchief, you gave me,
soaked in our tears, as I headed out for
the Big Ten Midwest. The only contents
of my safety deposit box, besides
the fragments of sky, pieces of stars: our
wedding rings: the ten coins from the blind cash-
ier at the White Sands' Missile Range Gift Shop—

ten years shaped into a friction drum, made
from the rosin fronds of willows that lined
Lock Lane, mountain biking past abandoned
cars and Celtic temples, me complaining
about the rough terrain. Ten years rubbed with
raspberry vodka and dilled baby corn;
scored by the rickety tap dance of wood
slats on Coney Island's Cyclone. Or scored
by the tap shoes we found in a seconds
store, the word "burnt" chalked on each sky-blue sole—

ten years: a rosewood circle tambourine,
you got to do more than bang it to make
it play, you said, one March morning, as we

ate bagels and watched the squirrels go crazy
making love outside. While above ten milk
orange clouds: a chain-link sky fence to guard the
angels: an overground listening device—
a couple naps side by side—up north whales
arrive at their feeding ground ten tundra
swans alighting on a cranberry bog—

ten years: *Is something wrong? No, no, nothing's
wrong. Are you sure? Sure, I'm sure nothing is
wrong. Nothing's wrong, really? Really. Okay,
but, you seem upset. No, I'm telling you
that nothing is wrong. If something was wrong
you would tell me? Wouldn't you? Was it me?
Did I do something to upset you? No,
nothing is wrong, nothing really. Are you
sure, obviously something's wrong. Really,
no, nothing's wrong. Okay, nothing is wrong.*

(Ten baby mermaids on a clam shell float
at the Coney Island Mermaid Parade,
Haitian drum-band mermaids, heavy metal
mermaids, a merman sheriff in lamé,
hockey playing topless purple mermaids,
a mermaid transfigured by chemical
waste, a mermaid accordion polka
band in a Cadillac, a beautiful
blue child mermaid in a blue chariot
pulled by her merdog dalmatian, Neptune.)

Ten years now, I guess there's no turning back,
there are some things I know we'll never do
again, like the subway conductor said,
*Watch out the doors are closing, the M and
the N the Q are passing:* halfway
down the alphabet: I'll never sit with
you in a cheap hotel room wearing nothing
but your cologne, joint file, or check the box
"married," or wear a string bikini: though
I won't rule out the possibility . . .

on the radio, Nelson Mandela
is president! Decalogues of light on
Lafayette and the Bowery's masonry—
reasons why it ended? I only think
of lying on a blanket decoding
the night sky, watching meteor showers,
of you telling me stories, I would say,
darling, please, tell me that story again:

ten years of tenacity, of blind faith
in the tenets of union; more often
attending to the manifest than the
latent; more often not asking the right
questions, as our main form of maintenance;
you thought sadness just came with the tenure.
Now it's over. And I'm still listening
at the red door trying to remember
why, looking for a portent in a bowl
of ten red steaming beets for what vanished—

ten years: and I remember more about
the trees we've seen: the bewitched and twisted
cypress made elegant by salt and wind;
aspens like ghosts snared by light: fenced ginkgoes
russet branches, musky leaves outside our
window at 44 Prospect Place: why
can I suddenly taste, the exact taste
of the air rowing out to the ruins
of a stone beach house and not remember
your taste? Was it almond or cilantro?

Ten reasons why it ended: because you
heard erase when I said grace; because I
heard broiled prawns when you said, let's do it
on the lawn; because my first course was your
race horse; when you said bird feeder I heard
lurid fingers; when you said frost bite I
heard moist delight; in your past tense I found
palimpsest; when you said please, I heard pass

the peas; when I said help yourself you heard
naked elf; we didn't know how to lis-

ten, because we didn't know how to ask
the right questions; because somewhere a house
was aflame; and just at this moment a
baby is made; because we recited
a sonnet by Keats as we walked across
the Brooklyn Bridge; because of the lost shards
locked in a suitcase on a Scottish plain;
because of summer and winter: and what's
found in between; because oceans and clouds—
yes, that's why, because of oceans and clouds—

from *TriQuarterly*

Perfect Attendance:
Short Subjects Made from
the Staring Photos of Strangers

◊ ◊ ◊

*The hand has its dreams, too, and its own hypotheses. It helps us to come to
know matter in its secret inward parts.*
—Gaston Bachelard

Suppose, in the old sense, they are waiting, expecting these loose silver frames
to dissolve in a million scenes, different every time and yet familiar, sponges

brought up from the dream floor, cuttings spliced into the blueing grain of
      closeup,
and careful backward steps toward the big picture, bringing what we can into
      view.

As when someone's Uncle Theo, his name the old Greek joke of "Uncle Uncle,"
misjudges his scythe-like sponge knife beneath the reef at Tarpon Springs

and bright red ribbons stream into this foreign sea from his bleeding hand,
the one that puts food on the table, and down in that pain he thinks of spring

and how his island blooms shore to shore, red poppies his grandfather told him
are every drop of blood ever shed in a war. If I've said this last before, forgive

what can't be said too many times. And, then, the hand that wears a crocheted
      glove
sometimes removes the glove and smokes, sometimes smokes with the glove

on, both years later and in another life, for the crocheted glove is first supremely
drawn to wild violets in a Texas pecan bottom on mornings still cool at seven,

violets set in a small pink glass at the bedside of the old woman who coughs
and will not come back, even a lifetime later when the crocheted gloves are
          bought

in a thrift shop and taken out dancing where women smoke. Such as an older
schoolmate named Olga whose right hand blurs at the register, this is the fifties

when the keys are round and rimmed with silver: dry beans, milk, thin tortillas,
she rings me up so fast, chimes the sum, left hand flashing a tiny diamond and

her long reach down the counter for a bag stop-framed over and over in the air,
a many-armed goddess who one day is not in school because her father has died

under a train in the roundhouse a few blocks away, his grease-streaked right
hand still clutching a wrench. What if finally neither art nor life is imitation,

and each waits everywhere, full-blown, but needing the gift of perfect attendance:
a twirling red skirt, work boots coated with clay mud, a weathered ladder left
          askew

near a pear tree in afternoon sun, basket nearby, whatever we cherish, we save.
Muybridge's incessant horses, the clock covering its mysterious face with its
          hands.

                        from *The Progressive*

Aeon Flux: June

◊   ◊   ◊

Not sibylline but clear, empty weather; of the eight kinds of sky it
was the milk-paled potion most like a cup of coffee she poured
past full in such a way as to show herself how good she was, how
the liquid lolled just over the white cup's rim, just so the instant
before an apology, until the surface broke and color seeming
singular though made of mix came sweetly over the sides after
which she could never think of herself as perfect again, falling
deeper into bright degradation as one falls down a well with
great relief, forgetting on the way how as a child she made her
father stop at every corner so she could sketch in her daybook
the cross street and what stores were where, using his back for a
desk. But he never forgot, he felt the markings each morning, a
ghost tattoo about her he couldn't stop describing to strangers: If
there is writing in this place, he begins, it's only proof that a tribe
of pens once lived here, pardoning themselves in advance for
their mortal leap from a line of thinking to a half-lit field which
starts under the rubric of hay and fruit trees but seems to contain
much more than mere space allows, in the vicinity of sundown
and all the nouns streaked with gold, drowning in drachmas,
lounging in louche, leading from the eye to the distant mountain
the guidebooks say is uninhabitable though behind it squats a
shack which is the summer home of God, finally free from
making cherries for the emperor's children; little God with his
funny name for which the other students teased him so, his
elaborate notes.

from *Ploughshares*

Litany

◇ ◇ ◇

You are the bread and the knife,
The crystal goblet and the wine . . .
—Jacques Crickillon

You are the bread and the knife,
the crystal goblet and the wine.
You are the dew on the morning grass
and the burning wheel of the sun.
You are the white apron of the baker
and the marsh birds suddenly in flight.

However, you are not the wind in the orchard,
the plums on the counter,
or the house of cards.
And you are certainly not the pine-scented air.
There is just no way you are the pine-scented air.

It is possible that you are the fish under the bridge,
maybe even the pigeon on the general's head,
but you are not even close
to being the field of cornflowers at dusk.

And a quick look in the mirror will show
that you are neither the boots in the corner
nor the boat asleep in its boathouse.

It might interest you to know,
speaking of the plentiful imagery of the world,
that I am the sound of rain on the roof.

I also happen to be the shooting star,
the evening paper blowing down an alley,
and the basket of chestnuts on the kitchen table.

I am also the moon in the trees
and the blind woman's tea cup.
But don't worry, I am not the bread and the knife.
You are still the bread and the knife.
You will always be the bread and the knife,
not to mention the crystal goblet and—somehow—
    the wine.

from *Poetry* and *Harper's*

Six Sketches:
When a Soul Breaks

◊　◊　◊

1. THE SPY

Years later, the house paid for, the church his rock, he was caught selling
his nation's secrets. The sudden silences, the sudden executions overseas
now had their explanation. A woman whose husband's cover
he'd blown tried to shoot him, failed, shot herself. Interviewed
in jail, he pleaded frustration, money problems, office politics:
"It got so bad I thought, 'the enemy can't be worse . . .' "

> *When a soul breaks*
> *There's no outward sign at first.*

2. THE HOOKER

Deborah, gorgeous, sixteen, could not decide which one was worse:
going home to mom and school and giving up Larry John, or selling
herself to buy a place as his woman. Arguments shook her, as politics
shake a statehouse. But a touch from him drove them into the seas.
After the knife fight with Mary Jack the Bear, Deborah, interviewed
about her rival's death, said: "I was freezing. Her blood was warm cover."

> *When a soul breaks, they say,*
> *The devil is its lover.*

3. THE POET

The poet, plotting suicide, planned to be found once more, to recover.
She'd written of her resurrection, and expected nothing worse
than a triumphant convalescence, Cerberus left whimpering, herself interviewed
anew by some severe psychiatrist. How could she have foreseen the selling
of her death, the secrets cracked like eggs, the word war across seas,
the perverse success of her plan to rout defeat, and mold the muse's politics?

> *When a soul breaks*
> *Triumph and folly are in the mix.*

4. THE MUSICIAN

The guitarist builds a city of air. With sidewinding feedback, pitch politics,
he drives democracy past the speed of sound. His blues riffs uncover
the will of the people: his overtones guide it arklike over seas. . . .
And born of doubt, that ark carries all: swindles, acid hits, power trips, worse-
than-flimsy philosophies—but also what the heavens are selling:
infinity in a gracenote, fulfillment rising up, the Mystery interviewed.

> *When a soul breaks all hail*
> *the voodoo tune that is debuted.*

5. THE PHILOSOPHER

His reason rode the centuries, probing beyond good and evil. It interviewed
the universe, plunged past creditor and debtor and mere politics.
But syphilis rode along, a monstrous link back to buying and selling,
to shyness and pride that left only a pain-drunk prostitute to cover
his hurt. As the books spilled out and idols trembled, the disease grew worse,
devoured his mind, plunged him in madness deep as the seas.

> *When a soul breaks,*
> *Accidents crush philosophies.*

6. MANIAS

Greed and skill can make a tulip worth more than the seven seas
or bring a storied bank crashing down, or topple a much-interviewed
CEO, leaving him rich with his word worth nothing. But worse,
some say, is purity, bright in the strongman's heart as the moon, shining politics
in place of gold, and sending thinker, poet and singer running for cover—
purity that leaves spy and pimp trading favors where selling

is banned: Purity of the moon-bright man of politics, interviewed,
selling again his old guerilla triumphs, and saying, "tighten belts! It's worse to
      cover
our battles with foreign credit, or throw bridges across protecting seas."

> *When a people's soul breaks, they say,*
> *the ruler raises his fees.*
>
> *And when a soul breaks,*
> *the devil is its lover.*
> *And triumph and folly are in the mix*
> *when a soul breaks.*
> *But there's no outward sign at first—*
> *until a voodoo tune gets debuted,*
> *and the ruler raises his fees,*
> *and accidents crush philosophies,*
> *and souls break.*

from *Callaloo*

World History

◇　◇　◇

Better to make oneself ridiculous by believing
Ten thousand angels can waltz on the head of a pin
And not feel crowded than believe it's time
For the armies of the Austro-Hungarian Empire
To teach the Serbs a lesson they'll never forget
For shooting the Archduke Ferdinand in Sarajevo.

Better to go door to door in Dusseldorf or Marseilles
And leave the taxpayers scratching their heads
At your report of a kingdom of heaven within them
Than argue it's time for Germany to display the fidelity
Of the German character to its Austrian kin,
Or time for France to honor its solemn promise
To side with Russia in defending Serbia from invasion,
Or ask if England should honor its word to France
Or give up thinking itself a gentleman.

To wonder, after a month without one convert,
If other people exist, if they share the world
That you inhabit, if you've merely dreamed them
To keep from feeling lonely—that's enough
To make the silence that falls when you stop preaching
Seem a valley of looming shadows.
But it can't compare to the silence of bristling nations
Standing toe to toe in a field, each army certain
It couldn't be anywhere else, given the need
Of great nations to be ready for great encounters.

And if it's hard to argue that spirit
Is anything more than a word when defined
As something separate from what is mortal,
It's easy to recognize the spirit of the recruit
Not convinced his honor has been offended
Who decides it's time to step from the line
And catch a train back to his cottage
Deep in the boondocks, where his wife and daughter
Are waiting to serve him supper and hear the news.

from *Poetry*

Skin

◊ ◊ ◊

And what are they to do with pieces of it that lie in the grass
or waft down afterwards, floating through the atmosphere

like feathers from a featherbed in the tale about the girl
who disappears down a well and returns

in a shower of gold? What to do
with all the minute pieces, the shreds?

The air at times turns violet, the sun neglects
to warm the grainy strip of sand we lie on

waiting to be touched and transformed. And the body
falls apart like hair unloosed, returns element to element,

distills itself. We are only bone and water after all.
Skin covers the gray-tinged grass like the oldest balm

to heal sickness. The air corrupts, dries it,
breaks it down into its former life of cells

to join the inert world of soil and leaf.
They say Da Vinci's molecules

still orbit the globe, that the air he breathed,
we breathe today. So that when blood is spilled

when skin rains down on this dry earth, perhaps
somehow, the earth remembers.

Jerusalem bombing, February 1996

from *Rhino*

Fox Trot Fridays

◇　◇　◇

Thank the stars there's a day
each week to tuck in

the grief, lift your pearls, and
stride brush stride

quick-quick with a
heel-ball-toe. Smooth

as Nat King Cole's
slow satin smile,

easy as taking
one day at a time:

one man and
one woman,

rib to rib,
with no heartbreak in sight—

just the sweep of Paradise
and the space of a song

to count all the wonders in it.

from *Callaloo*

Open Door Blues

◇ ◇ ◇

The male wild turkey in the field
is all puffed up and unfurled.
Pecking at the ground, absorbed,
the female doesn't seem to care;
no sex, she seems to be saying,
before food. He looks the fool.
Cool air since you've been gone.
I haven't touched the heat, yet
the baseboard heaters are pinging
an atonal song. Balanced on its
haunches, your rocking chair
isn't rocking anymore. It can't,
alone, be fully what it is. I've
given it every one of its thoughts.
It thinks you'll not return.
The creature that's burrowed
inside the wall, probably a squirrel,
is chewing something with bones.
Every time I kick the spot,
it stops, but not for long.
It seems to believe it can't be hurt.
I've left the door open. The flies
know. The wasps soon will.

from *Brilliant Corners*

Journal

◊   ◊   ◊

In a dream journal kept as an experiment,
evidence of a life that went
on without him while he slept, salvaged
fragments that might yield revelations
about the past or future, he found himself
recording nights they spent together.

On a page of frozen landscape
across which he towed his father,
now shrunk into a child, on a sled
meant to transport a dead battery,
was the August night she'd wiped
their sweat with unbound hair.

Rowing a turbulent sea of doors,
he woke to tingle of wings, a bat
brushing the wind chime in her room,
and hovering lips alighting along
the length of his body. He was lost
on a shore where clarinets were

driftwood, and sunrise a camisole
slipped from her shoulder. Each time
she came, she cried; erect nipples
tasting of tears, earlobes familiar
with their taste of pearls.
The mortgage on his soul was down

to a dollar but where to pay it off?
Baby, she said, we're practicing
kissing interruptus. To save the world
from humankind, a desperate cabal
of cetaceans merged the psychic power
of their enormous brains.

His handprint still emblazoned
on her ass as she stepped into the shower.
Prisoners of war, assigned a classroom
in which to await decapitation,
sat passively at fifth-grade desks
while he paced wishing for a gun,

and when the executioners rushed in
it was another night in which the choice
was death or starting from the dream.
3 A.M. He lay listening to her breath,
wondering should he gently wake her
with his tongue, or let her sleep.

from *Tin House*

The Vagrant Hours

◊ ◊ ◊

September

The month of sonnets:
The long distance runners roamed the hills
recited their poems in the afternoon and kissed.
The poet-professor in corduroy cuffed pants
daydreamed of his evening flask of black whiskey
his nightwatch over the hourglass of metaphors.
The young man was cumbersome in his stall.

October

The month of sestinas:
The charm of lovers against the burred ivy walls
held the riddle of sixes and coaxed the student's heart
to a blackboard of pentagrams and tarot flames in chalk.
The griot's basket of apples, chestnuts, and maple leaves
held back the screen door of their teacher's writing studio.
Did she hide the laurel wild under her skirt?

November

The month of villanelles:
The young poet nods off in the back of the classroom
and a wooden pointer curled the cowlick on his head.
He was made to stand before the assembly and sing.

With long shadows and wings of the runners on the hill
into November's end and the town clock's vagrant hour
he lowered his head and begged a rhyme scheme for love.

December

The month of elegies:
They held the widow's wreath and opulent arms of death
healed the child's thumb that broke out of a wool mitten.
They waited under a rain of taps and six-gun salute
for the son to place his hand on his father's cheek
for the wry minister to rise from his narrow chair
and place the widow's glove and ring into the urn.

January

The month of blank verse:
They say he tracked a wounded animal
drop for drop for three and a half damn weeks
broke its long neck bare-handed dead and stirred
right strong coffee until he heard noises.
The hot prairie wind howled a fancy tune.
He knew it was a way of knowing things.

February

The month of ballads and woe:
The traveler brings a small gift to her screen door
and he barely remembers the song she whispered
sixteen years before under the lilac covered bridge.
Was that her low voice rising above the top of trees
or a meteor with its own articulation of the heavens
in the arc of falling embers that filled the brown field?

March

The month of pantoums:
She stood for hours in mud
for a handsome young man
who turned into a beer slug
not a fine bottle of wine.

For a handsome young man
who turned into a beer slug
not a fine bottle of wine
she stood for hours in mud.

April

The month of odes and affliction:
This was not the cruelest month Mr. Eliot
until a letter arrived out of nowhere from an old friend
the best damned drinking captain twenty-six years ago.
He wrote down poems that spent his failing heart
a hunger of gravity removed from the chest cavity.
He was on a waiting list for love and a new heart.

May

The month of heroic couplets:
Let there be thunder in his heart again
let a church bell's echo dance in his pen!
Where he erred once let him live twice
as he lived once let him parry twilight.
Let his breath shape the hourglass
and the last sailboat raise its mast!

June

The month of pastorals:
The poet met Art Pierce cliff-side at *Ojo Caliente*
a calligrapher of sandhill cranes in clay and arsenic
sent by the god of letters to the underworld spring.
They lifted their chalices to the crippled and mortal
who swam the miracle waters for the unkind rebirth
who sought refuge in the ghost chamber of the earth.

July

The month of stanzas:
This was the month of writer's block.
Nothing moved his fingers on the typewriter
until rain outside his studio in the burnt sky
formed a rainbow in the watchmaker's eyepiece.
There landed on his bad shoulder a poor white raven
found in his good hand a ruby from the baker's oven.

August

The month of *verse libre:*
The poet learned to dance inside forms
as feather and ink spread over the pages
one misspelled word in the spelling bee.
He studied the burial ground of images
how love was subtle and hidden in a line
how love was metered and love was rare.

from *Mississippi Review*

Ponderosa

◇   ◇   ◇

It was out in the middle of the light, no way back for that old giant.

Other trees stood cloaked at a safe distance.
                                    I used to think its
name meant it was thoughtful.
                                    It did look like a green brain on a
stem, alive in wind.
                        I thought it got emotions from its roots in
earth, intelligence from needles in the sun.
                                    I thought it must make
sense of everything.
                        Basque shepherds carved their love poems in
its bark and cut Lascaux-like glyphs of antelope and girls.
                                                    Those
Basques—Matisses of the plains, gouging desires into a thinking
tree that seemed to come striding over the horizon, like a verdant
thunderhead, mushroom cloud of true benignity.
                                                    Sooner or later, we
all knew, lightning had to strike, and when it did we saw it.
                                                    The bolt
came down like knowledge, but the tree did not explode or burn.
                                                                    It
caught the jolt and trapped it like a mythic girl.
                                                    Its trunk was three
feet through.
                Lightning couldn't blow the ponderosa into splinters,
and couldn't burn inside without some air.
                                    A week went by and we

forgot about it.

                        But lightning is a very hot and radiant girl.

                                           When
heat bled out to bark, the tree burst into flame that reared into
silence under a cloudless sky.

                        Brain of ash, what can you tell me
now?

      What were your thoughts, concerning history?

          from *Boston Review*

AMY GERSTLER

An Offer Received
in This Morning's Mail:

(On misreading an ad for a set of CDs entitled
"Beethoven's Complete Symphonies.")

◇   ◇   ◇

The Musical Heritage Society
invites you to accept
Beethoven's Complete Sympathies.
A full $80.00 value, yours for $49.95.
The brooding composer
of "Ode to Joy" now delighting
audiences in paradise nightly
knows your sorrows. Just look
at his furrowed brow, his thin
lipped grimace. Your sweaty
2 am writhings have touched
his great Teutonic heart. Peering
invisibly over your shoulder
he reads those poems you scribble
on memo pads at the office,
containing lines like *o lethal blossom,*
I am your marionette forever,
and a compassionate smile trembles
at the corners of his formerly stern
mouth. (He'd be thrilled to set
your poems to music.) This immortal
master, gathered to the bosom

of his ancestors over a century ago
has not forgotten those left behind
to endure gridlock and mind-ache,
wearily crosshatching the earth's surface
with our miseries, or belching complaints
into grimy skies, further besmirching
the firmament. But just how relevant
is Beethoven these days, you may ask.
Wouldn't the sympathies of a modern
composer provide a more up-to-date
form of solace? Well, process this info-byte,
21st century skeptic. A single lock
of Beethoven's hair fetched over $7,000
last week at auction. The hairs were then
divided into lots of two or three and resold
at astronomical prices. That's how significant
he remains today. Beethoven the great-hearted,
who used to sign letters *ever thine,*
the unhappiest of men, wants you
to know how deeply sorry he is
that you're having such a rough time.
Prone to illness, self-criticism
and squandered affections—
Ludwig (he'd like you to call him that,
if you'd do him the honor,)
son of a drunk and a depressive,
was beaten, cheated, and eventually
went stone deaf. He too had to content
himself with clutching his beloved's
tooth-marked yellow pencils
(as the tortured scrawls in his notebooks
show) to sketch out symphonies, concerti,
chamber music, etcetera—works
that still brim, as does your disconsolate
soul, with unquenched fire and brilliance.
Give Beethoven a chance to show
how much he cares. Easy financing
available. And remember:

a century in heaven has not calmed
the maestro's celebrated temper, so act now.
For god's sake don't make him wait.

from *American Poetry Review*

Landscape

◇   ◇   ◇

Time passed, turning everything to ice.
Under the ice, the future stirred.
If you fell into it, you died.

It was a time
of waiting, of suspended action.

I lived in the present, which was
that part of the future you could see.
The past floated above my head,
like the sun and moon, visible but never reachable.

It was a time
governed by contradictions, as in
I felt nothing and
I was afraid.

Winter emptied the trees, filled them again with snow.
Because I couldn't feel, snow fell, the lake froze over.
Because I was afraid, I didn't move;
my breath was white, a description of silence.

Time passed, and some of it became this.
And some of it simply evaporated;
you could see it float above the white trees
forming particles of ice.

All your life, you wait for the propitious time.
Then the propitious time
reveals itself as action taken.

I watched the past move, a line of clouds moving
from left to right or right to left,
depending on the wind. Some days

there was no wind. The clouds seemed
to stay where they were,
like a painting of the sea, more still than real.

Some days the lake was a sheet of glass.
Under the glass, the future made
demure, inviting sounds;
you had to tense yourself so as not to listen.

Time passed; you got to see a piece of it.
The years it took with it were years of winter;
they would not be missed. Some days

there were no clouds, as though
the sources of the past had vanished. The world

was bleached, like a negative; the light passed
directly through it. Then
the image faded.

Above the world
there was only blue, blue everywhere.

from *The Threepenny Review*

Report on Human Beings

◇   ◇   ◇

You know about desks and noses,
proteins, mortgages, orchestras,
nationalities, contraceptives;
you have our ruins and records,
but they won't tell you
what we were like.

We were distinguished
by our interest in scenery;
we could look at things for hours
without using or breaking them—
and there was a touch of desperation, not to be found
in any other animal,
in the looks of love we directed
at our children.

We were treacherous of course.
Like anything here—
winds, dogs, the sun—
we could turn against you unexpectedly,
we could let you down.
But what was remarkable about us
and which you will not believe
is that we alone,
with the exception of a few pets
who probably learned it from us,
when betrayed
were frequently surprised.

We were one of a million species
who continually cried out
or silently wept with pain.
I am proud that we alone resented
taking part in the chorus.

Yes, some of us
liked to cause pain.
Yes, most of us
sometimes
liked to cause pain,
but I am proud that most of us
were ashamed
afterward.

Our love of poetry would have amused you;
we were so proud of language
we thought we invented it
(and thus failed to notice
the speech of animals,
the birds' repeated warnings,
the whispered intelligence
of mutant cells).

We did invent boredom,
a fruitful state.
It hid the size of our desires.
We were spared many murders,
many religions
because we could say, "I am bored."
A kind of clarity
came when we said it
and we could go to Paris or the movies,
give useful parties, master languages,
rather than sink our teeth in our lover's throat
and shake till things felt right again.

Out of the same pulsing world
you know,
out of gases, whorls,

fronds, feelers, jellies,
we devised hard edges,
strings of infinite tension stretched
to guide us.
The mind's pure snowflake
was our map.
Lines, angles, outlines
not to be found in rocks or seas
or living matter
or in the holes of space,
how strange these shapes must look to you,
at odds with everything,
uncanny, broken from the flow,
I think they must be for you
what we called art.

What was most wonderful about us
was our kindness,
but of this it is impossible to speak.
Only someone who knows our cruelty,
who knows the fears we always lived with,
fear of inside and outside, smooth and rough,
soft and hard, wet and dry, touch and no touch,
only someone who understands the great palace we built
on the axis of time
out of our fear and cruelty and called history,
only those who have lived in the anger
of a great modern city,
who saw the traffic in the morning
and the police at night
can know how heartbreaking
our kindness was.

Let me put it this way.
One of us said, "I think
our life is not as good
as the mind warrants,"
another, "It is hard

to be alone and alive at the same time."
To understand these statements
you would have to be human.

Our destruction as a species
was accidental.
Characteristically
we blamed it on ourselves,
which neither the eagle
nor the dinosaur would do.

Look closely around you,
study your instruments,
scan the night sky.
We were alien.
Nothing in the universe
resembles us.

from *Ontario Review*

RAY GONZALEZ

Max Jacob's Shoes

◇   ◇   ◇

They were found after his death by someone who needed shoes. When this man plucked them out of a mountain of trash, Max Jacob's shoes came alive. They fit this person as if truth had never left and he slowly walked away from the filth. It took him a few days to realize he wore the shoes of a poet. The black shoelaces started talking to him in his sleep, the poems drifting out at night, floating beyond the man's bed to recite themselves to life. Max Jacob's black shoes glistened as if they had been shined yesterday, the sleepy man looking over the edge of his bed as the talking shoes tapped a clicking message that said a man who wears someone else's shoes is a man who knows how to get along in life. When he put them on in the early light of dawn, the shoes quit reciting poetry and led the man to a quiet church Jacob never would have entered. The new owner of the shoes went into a church for the first time in over thirty years, the shoes echoing across the silent sanctuary where a surprised priest waited, sensing the approach of Jewish shoes. After the stranger revealed his sins to the priest, he emerged from the dark confessional and looked down at his bare feet. He went back into the tiny chamber, but Max Jacob's shoes were gone, their hushed disappearance casting a steady light of awareness on the barefoot man, the helpless priest, even the two mice in the sanctuary who revealed themselves to no one that night as they busily gnawed on a pair of twisted shoelaces.

from *New American Writing*

LINDA GREGG

Beauty

◇ ◇ ◇

There she was on Entertainment Tonight.
Someone had caught a glimpse of Bardot
after all these years. Brigitte Bardot
running through the trees, across a meadow,
a dog running with her. The hair still long.
Then another part showing her on the patio,
aged. (Sun-damaged, we say.) The violation
of beauty never happens just once.
When my father heard his beloved dog
had chased and killed the rancher's sheep,
he went right out and shot it. Because,
he said, once they ran with the pack
and tasted blood it would never stop.

from *The New Yorker*

The Opaque

◇   ◇   ◇

We crave it because we feel it is secretly us
after the ideas wearing name-tags have had their
        big convention.
But that's an idea; that's not it.

Bumpy muddy fields with stands of scruffy trees.

Blueprints for the wiring of public buildings in Singapore.

The life lived in a purple Volkswagen
parked next to the Almstead Tree Company in New Rochelle.

A quick-stepping woman in a corridor, moving away;
her calves.

In the opaque, there are only examples.

Venezuela.

Any one word said over and over. Opaque.

Ed Skoog. Opaque. Mitch Green. Opaque.
Serina Mammon. Out of reach.

Gusto of deer hunters. Venison draining.

Speckly smudged static of when we are too tired, when are we
too tired for one more example?

Seventy-year-old twins who sing together of baby Jesus.

Juliette Gréco singing at Le Boeuf Sur Le Toit
and how some guy named Bernard interpreted her phrasing.
Years back, years back years back.

Hundreds of people standing in rain to watch golf.

The next thing, the next thing you get stuck on
before it becomes a handy metaphor . . .

A news item in Arabic about stolen bicycles.

If there were a tribe of Indians called the Opakis,
their way of stitching beaver pelts would be opaque.

Those gray people politely serving around the edges
of your life and how they can stand it.

Bumpy muddy fields with stands of scruffy trees
and why the trees bother to stand up.

Silence of a stuffed bag of laundry.
Laundry, laundry.

That blonde woman on the subway, she wasn't Sophie
she couldn't have been Sophie

Cheddar cheese soup

The waitress who served me my cheddar cheese soup today
without a word and walked out of the restaurant
ten minutes later in her gray-blue winter jacket

The pain of that person you said you loved six years ago.

We get tired, but what would it mean to be tired enough?

Congested heart of a man committing murder
this very hour in Tennessee
(not yet a character in a novel).

What peels away from or pokes out through yesterday's
poem, poamb, poeem, pom-pom
in that black behind black ink . . .

Tintex—Japalac—
Kish & Sons Electric. Zelda's Diner.
Combo Basket at the Big Top.

Mister Thasildar of Bombay ignoring three young
dying prostitutes in a parlor of his Naazma bordello.

Beans in the middle of the night.

Who built this tunnel? How long is this tunnel?
Does it go somewhere? Oh never mind,
here comes the light of day.

from *Colorado Review*

Rhythmic Arrangements
(on prosody)

◊ ◊ ◊

I was forced to memorize and recite
in front of an atonal white hostess

made to do it again in itemized lists
on Iowa tests in critical argot complicit

with theatrical endrhymes adrift caesuras
worrying the line of nothing in the gut

but worried by the count in country
and out when Auden's "memorable speech"

came forward in softshoe slippers
librettos in tone deaf strife was no self

hidden in structures of spite
no sex could congress and no respite

from antics of song the pentameter
sometimey syllabics/accentuals

betraying the throttle and trestle
of the bridge, choral elements spared

in the wrestle of hesitant speech
so sprung rhythmaticals of geechytimbred

voice you carried as a load from slavery
certainly as if Elizabethan antics

of crosskeys in upper registers a drone
to find motherly lode commingles

on the vertical the increments implode
as horizontal keyboards of a scene

the metaphysics of the theorists
enjamb at exegesis

of human standards which reflect
alternatives to genuflection

I was an altarboy to blooming Joyce
the hymnal broken in makeshift storefronts

who brought the spirit low on high
"guess I'll give it one mo' try"

in a moment's notice you compose
wrangling halfnotes magical phrasings

in a voice lost/found in subway grids
handmade librarians of the heart and ids

from *LUNA*

Sad Little Breathing Machine

◇　◇　◇

Engine:@

Under its glass lid, the square
of cheese is like any other element

of the imagination—cough in the tugboat,
muff summering somewhere in mothballs.

Have a humbug. The world is slow
to dissolve & leave us. Is it your

hermeneut's helmet not letting me
filter through? The submarine sinks

with a purpose: Scientist Inside
Engineering A Shell. & meanwhile

I am not well. Don't know how to go on
Oprah without ya. On t.v., a documentary

about bees—yet another box in a box.
The present is in there somewhere.

from *Verse*

Villanelle

◇   ◇   ◇

(Spielberg visited an inner city school in response to a class of black students who had laughed inappropriately at a showing of his movie about the holocaust Schindler's List.*)*

When Steven Spielberg spoke at Oakland High
A custodian swept up the shattered glass,
replaced the broken clocks to satisfy

the Governor, who was preoccupied
with becoming President, with covering his ass.
When Steven Spielberg spoke at Oakland High

the District found diminishing supplies
of disinfectant and toilet paper stashed
away, so they replaced the clocks instead to satisfy

the cameras and the press that they had rectified
the deficiencies among the underclass.
When Steven Spielberg spoke at Oakland High

the students didn't seem dissatisfied
about the cover up, just happy to be out of class.
The custodian replaced the broken clocks to satisfy

this need we have to falsify
the truth in subservience to cash.
When Steven Spielberg came to Oakland High
the custodian replaced the broken clocks.

from *88*

EDWARD HIRSCH

The Desire Manuscripts

◇ ◇ ◇

I. THE CRAVING
The Odyssey, Book Twelve

I needed a warning from the goddess
and a group of men to lash me to the mast
hand and foot, so that I could listen
to swelling, sun-scorched, fatal voices
of two Sirens weaving a haunted sound
over the boiling surf, calling me downward
while I twisted with desire in the ropes
and pleaded to be untied, unbound, unleashed.
How willingly I would have given myself up
to that ardor, that drowning blue charm,
while hopeless clouds scudded overhead
and the deaf oarsmen rowed ruthlessly home.
I was saved, I know, but even now, years later,
I crave those voices dreaming in my sleep.

II. THE RAVISHMENT
The Odyssey, Book Twelve

I listened so the goddess could charm my mind
against the ravishing sunlight, the lord of noon,
and I could stroll through country unharmed
toward the prowling straits of Scylla and Charybdis,

but I was unprepared for the Siren lolling
on a bed in a dirty room above a tavern
where workers guzzled sour red wine
and played their cards late into the night.

It takes only a moment to cruise eternity
who dressed quickly and left, after twenty minutes,
taking my money. I went back to the ship
and the ordinary men pressing for home,

but, love, some part of me has never left
that dark green shore sweetened with clover.

III. WHAT THE GODDESS CAN DO
The Odyssey, Book Ten

Maybe it was the way she held her head
or her voice, which was too high, or her braids,
which reminded me of a girl I used to know,

but I sat on a tall chair like a god
drinking a bowl of honey mulled with wine
and getting drowsy, counting my good fortune,

so that she could transform me into a pig
squealing for acorns, grunting and bristling
in a sty, snouting the ground with other swine.

Later, our leader convinced her to reverse
the spell, setting our animal bodies free . . .

I have been many things in this life—
a husband, a warrior, a seer—but I cannot forget
what the goddess can do to me, if she desires.

IV. THE SENTENCE
Inferno, Canto Five

When you read Canto Five aloud last night
in your naked, singsong, fractured Italian,
my sweet compulsion, my carnal appetite,

I suspected we shall never be forgiven
for devouring each other body and soul,
and someday Minos, a connoisseur of sin,

will snarl himself twice around his tail
to sentence us to life in perpetual motion,
funneling us downward to the second circle

where we will never sleep or rest again
in turbulent air, like other ill-begotten
lovers who embraced passion beyond reason,

and yet I cannot turn from you, my wanton;
our heaven will always be our hell, a swoon.

V. THE MOURNING FIELDS
The Aeneid, Book Six

The world below is starless, stark and deep,
and while you lay beside me, my golden bough,
plunged into the shadowy marsh of sleep,

I read about the infernal realm, and how
a soldier walked forth in the House of Dis
while still alive, breaking an eternal law

by braving death's kingdom, a vast abyss,
the ground sunken in fog—eerie, treacherous—
guarded by a mad beast, three-throated Cerberus.

Tonight I read about us—foundering, hopeless—
in the Mourning Fields and the myrtle grove,
wandering on separate paths, lost in darkness.

It is written that we were consumed by love,
here on earth, a pitiless world above.

VI. AFTER ALL THE ORPHIC ENCHANTMENTS
The Metamorphoses, Books Ten and Eleven

After all the Orphic enchantments, after all
was said and done, after a second death stunned
and claimed his wife for the fluttering clouds
and phantom forms, the misting lower depths,

after he pleaded with Charon for a second chance
but was dismissed and chased above ground
where he shunned women for a good three years
and notched a life for himself with young men,

a vegetarian priest who recited the passions
of lovers who paid for their transgressions—
the Cerastes, the Propoetides, Pygmalion,
Myrrha and Cinyras, Venus and Adonis—

after everything was closed, completed,
and the costs were tallied, after he sang
for the hyacinths and virgin laurels
and charmed the drooling souls of beasts,

after he enraged the Thracian women who
circled like birds of prey and ripped him
into pieces, as the gods had prophesied,
after his body watered the ground with blood

and currents carried his severed head chanting
downstream with such a spellbinding grief
that trees shed leafy crowns and stones leapt
up and swollen rivers wept in their beds,

I wonder if Orpheus ever decided it was
worth it after all, relinquishing his body
so he could return to the nether world
which he knew by heart and where, I hope,

he moves with Eurydice on the other side,
a shade still singing amid the other shades,
sometimes walking behind her, sometimes ahead,
and swiveling round to gaze at her forever.

VII. THE REGRET

The Lost Orphics

If we had never married, if you had never strolled
barefoot through high grass with a poisonous snake
that sent you weeping alone into the underworld

to join the other shades, the fresh new recruits
arriving at all hours at the way station of eternity,
Persephone's insubstantial realm, the House of Death,

and if I, who could entrance the Stygian fog
and convince the god of our ravishing need for
each other, here and now, in the world above,

had never turned back for my limping wife
on a shadowy path out of utter silence,
the void of Avernus, the margins of earth,

then I might not be floating here alone
on a mournful hillside, devoid of shade,
praising young boys beloved by the fates

to the approaching trees, the bright lotus,
lover of pools, and the bittersweet hazel,
the river-haunted willow and the mountain ash,

awaiting my own death, the crazed Furies
who will send my head and my lyre downstream
still singing about us, what might have been.

from *The Paris Review*

Summer Night

◇ ◇ ◇

That one night in the middle of the summer
when people move their TV sets outside
and watch them on the porch—
so the neighborhood is full of murmuring blue lights.

Earlier, the evening sky looked like a pale blue shirt
through which a stain the shade of watermelon juice
was delicately spreading.

All day I kept offering my wife
opportunities to fight,
and she kept stepping over them
like cracks in a sidewalk she was used to walking on.

Sometimes when she cries I think how
cigarettes and ice cream are part
of the chemical composition of her tears,

sometimes I think about her mom and dad,
her catastrophic history with men—
And I can feel the roots of my heart

convulse, yanking themselves up, wanting to
walk over there and hold her.

We sit in our wooden chairs,
convinced that we have ruined everything

while through the open window
comes the smell of flowers.

from *88*

Success

◊   ◊   ◊

Her dealer, who handled successful artists,
   was a successful dealer,
and his Christmas party, too, was a success:

we all knew it, for weren't we all there?
   And the successful artist
being handled in her eighth decade knew it

too, although she was so old and had been so
   unsuccessful for so long
that she seemed to pay no mind to anyone.

She sat quite still, her rosy scalp glistening
   through her rather thin white hair,
and gave no sign of hearing, or ignoring,

any of our successful conversations.
   Above the chair she sat in
(like a furnished bone) loomed the decorative

focus of the long room which had been handled
   by a successful designer
of skeletal interiors: a Roman male,

oversize and barely under overweight,
   every muscle equally
successful—classically nude but not

in the least naked as any man would be.
   And as the talk continued
Alice Neel leaned back and looked up into

the forking limbs above her head, a pure
   pelvic arch indeed denuded
of the usual embellishment, so that

all that met her eye was a shadowed empty
   socket, the mere embouchure
where once unstinting paraphernalia

must have lodged. "Very fragile things, penises,"
   she mused, and for a moment
no one there succeeded in saying a word.

   from *The New Yorker*

Ten Sighs from a Sabbatical

◇ ◇ ◇

1

Let loose. Lists into ashes. Tasks into stones.
In lethargy I revise myself. I loiter in the lily's canal.
Time to mood-walk among obsolete resolutions.
To drain rhetoric to all that does not speak and cannot listen.
Hello thistle. What do horses hear?
A nap cleans me like a tooth. Mere duty rocks the hours.
The brain's self-whispering brushes the conscious event.
The face of a good friend is a breast.
A call comes in on the switchboard of the birds.
I swivel and skitter, a potato thrown through a warehouse.
I am injected with dream questions.
Instruct me, heavenly recipe for the worms.
How long must I be buried before I am done?
Rub me right, rule me, sweet other.
I'm old wood and new string.
I can only be an animal through this violin.

2

Who speaks now as if subject and predicate decree the world?
The trees were locked up, but have broken out.
I trail off down the sidewalk of an afterthought,
Only a busted cycle Lord, a gleam spirited to rust.
What litters of darkness televisions own.
I'm a punched ticket swaddled by lint.
Come eavesdroppers, hear the foreplay of obsessions.

A tsk-tsking, with a dumpty-do for variation.
Who else sits here, blues-measled, lonesome afternoons,
looking up follicle and Warren G. Harding
in *Compton's Illustrated Encyclopedia?*
Are you better than once, lightest foreshadowing?
Are you the largest amygdala in homeroom?

3

Pilgrim, what good there is for you to see
finds you. You don't have to look for it.
A lily trembles by a spring-fed brook.
Live children dream. A tax accountant
does a glum impression of Charlie Chan.
I'm off this year, dally to your dilly, yang
to your yin, but let me visit the office
once, friends open their mouths
to show the scars of humorectomies.
Why? Who's not wronged? Go cut a switch,
my own sweet mama used to say, and me
I'd bring back a reed while my smarter
sister would present a gnarl of thorns.
But there's a glitch in utter victimhood.
The wronged-by-men-and-women face down
the wronged-by-God. Walk fast or run.
All verse-writers moan, *Too late,* and presto!
We're poster children for the post-irony telethon.

4

But oh to have come up with something new
a minor amendment to a hairdo,
a twitch in a phrase, or chevron on shirt.
The will of others must be sidestepped after all.
If one is to reach into the pocket and bring up
like a magician's rabbit, the gold eggs of the future,
one needs a tongue-ring, earring, or mustache,
though in the case of bards, what dumb malaise

and spiritual laryngitis leaves may only be
the aboard-saying panic and subliminal love sigh
of the greased consonants turning among vowels.
"Stretch out," they seem to say, "lay it all down
here in the seeds of the twenty-first century,
in the United States of America," and, "baby, baby."

5

The great man, head like a cauliflower, addressed our poems
Thursday mornings, pontificating between coughing jags.
And what he said: "History includes you in this small way,"
and what he meant: "Don't wake me up."
He who had sat with Cummings, Hart Crane, and Pound.

And what he remembered of all his time with Eliot:
"He never said anything stupid. He never made a mistake."

"Why are you doing this?" I asked the one time we were alone.
"I'm giving my wife a horse or a swimming pool."

Cummings was a gentleman. Pound was genuinely batty
and believed himself Christ. Randall was jealous of Cal.
"Cal should be exonerated for what he's writing now."

He skewered Mallarmé: "a short poet with a long tail."
Then hacked at himself, canning the horse in laugh.

He liked my poems best. Not much. I asked one other thing:

"After all these years, and books, what do you think of poetry?"

"I loathe and detest it."

6

The dead, when they are recent, are as good
as they will ever be. They do not bicker
or take the biggest share. They lie in state,
as well-groomed and polite as ambassadors.
Tired of the future, they lie down in the past.
Soon enough, it will be different, heavenly host:
God's moles, God's worms, God's nematodes,
Gabriels and St. Peters of putrefaction: hello.
Meat blooms wit; the vegetable maintenance
requires them. But now an interlude. Now,
as never in elegies, the living prefer the living.

7

My father, for all my childhood, would object
as others might oppose profanity, my sighs.
If I had finished splitting a pile of logs
or loading a truck of hay into the barn,
I only had to lean back, inhale a great gulp
of air and expel it with an undiminished whew
and there he was like Marcus Aurelius.
Oh I held tight, but now I give out
and go down the cleansing breath
dead-legged and bath-headed with joy.

8

Let loose. Lists into ashes. Tasks into stones.
Do the dead still dispatch scouts? Only
lunatics see angels. Surrealism's old-timey.
After fifty the men in my family doze off,
even passionately making a point, intensity
of eyes coming down on you like a wake—
you start to answer, and we're off

in the slack-jawed, log-sawing sublime.
This clear gift descends on us like water.
Thunder brings out our highest power.

9

Release is better than ecstasy, downglide
peeled from the resistance of the living,
sockfoot in the meridian of twilight.
What picked the brain like a morel?
The honesty of things calls silently. Minutes
of committee meetings, doodlings
and scribblings are the soul's holy writ.
The rain says, go and study with the birds.

10

It doesn't take much. Beautiful platitude:
All is delusion. In the right dark,
and if you are ignorant, brother,
a goose sounds like a coyote.
I'm looking for something a wren will approve.
One leak from the unlockable sea.
What's truer than fiction when it moves?
The peach in my own armflesh
makes me an agent of the sublime.

from *Five Points*

Some Rain

◇　◇　◇

Freud saw his first patient on a gray morning in Vienna;
cobblestones glistened feebly.
And it was pouring as Pollock dragged red onto *Full Fathom Five*.
Patty Hearst's face was grainy and soft, on closed-circuit,
as if we were watching her through a wet screen door,
but Socrates, as he died, looked sharply into the distance.
Early evening. Water coursed the gutters.
Remember the morning after, when Benjamin Franklin
did nothing in particular?
And how light loved the wipers on the bus to Selma?
Showers ruffled the Potomac as the burglars
were led over the Watergate lawn;
you could hear horses plashing as Galileo upended his telescope
to peer at the enormous, hairy legs of a housefly.
Watson, come here, I need you. Drops clung to the railings,
ran over the roof in thin streams.
In a soaking mist, the Lusitania gently sank;
bicycles stood in the rain as the students left Tiananmen Square.
The Lindbergh baby vanished through a wet, streaked window.
A few pale-green leaves were stuck to it.
Jane Eyre came back to find Rochester fumbling in a storm,
the yard full of fallen branches.
The tulip market crashed during a terrible downpour
but oxen grazed patiently at Lascaux, not minding.
If, as Hitler was declared chancellor, the crowd opened their umbrellas,
people stood barefoot in the mud sometimes at Birkenau.
The banality of evil, Hannah Arendt wrote, crushed out her cigarette
and got up to shut the windows.
As Marie Curie set out a small, glowing dish of radium

with her poisoned fingers, a line of storms was moving east;
faintly it thundered while my grandparents listened,
for the first time, to a phonograph.
Lewis Carroll wrote Alice onto the riverbank
while he floated downstream. The first drops were falling;
it was cool and still as the morning Alaric sacked Rome
or the one—it was June—Dickinson looked out at the grass
and said—something. What? Now that was some rain.

from *Pleiades*

The Dragon

◇ ◇ ◇

The bees came out of the junipers, two small swarms
The size of melons; and golden, too, like melons,
They hung next to each other, at the height of a deer's breast
Above the wet black compost. And because
The light was very bright it was hard to see them,
And harder still to see what hung between them.
A snake hung between them. The bees held up a snake,
Lifting each side of his narrow neck, just below
The pointed head, and in this way, very slowly
They carried the snake through the garden,
The snake's long body hanging down, its tail dragging
The ground, as if the creature were a criminal
Being escorted to execution or a child king
To the throne. I kept thinking the snake
Might be a hose, held by two ghostly hands,
But the snake was a snake, his body green as the grass
His tail divided, his skin oiled, the way the male member
Is oiled by the female's juices, the greenness overbright,
The bees gold, the winged serpent moving silently
Through the air. There was something deadly in it,
Or already dead. Something beyond the report
Of beauty. I laid my face against my arm, and there
It stayed for the length of time it takes two swarms
Of bees to carry a snake through a wide garden,
Past a sleeping swan, past the dead roses nailed
To the wall, past the small pond. And when
I looked up the bees and the snake were gone,
But the garden smelled of broken fruit, and across
The grass a shadow lay for which there was no source,

A narrow plinth dividing the garden, and the air
Was like the air after a fire, or before a storm,
Ungodly still, but full of dark shapes turning.

from *New England Review*

When the Towers Fell

◇　◇　◇

From our high window we saw the towers
with their bands and blocks of light
brighten against a fading sunset,
saw them at any hour glitter and live
as if the spirits inside them sat up all night
calculating profit and loss, saw them reach up
and steep their tops in the first yellow
of sunrise, grew so used to them
often we didn't see them, and now,
not seeing them, we see them.

The banker is talking to London.
Humberto is delivering breakfast sandwiches.
The trader is already working the phone.
The mail sorter has started sorting the mail.

> . . . *povres et riches*
> *Sages et folz, prestres et laiz*
> *Nobles, villains, larges et chiches*
> *Petiz et grans et beaulx et laiz . . .*

The plane screamed low down lower Fifth Avenue,
lifted at the Arch, someone said, shaking the dog walkers
in Washington Square Park, drove for the north tower,
struck with a heavy thud, released a huge bright gush
of blackened fire, and vanished, leaving a hole
the size and shape a cartoon plane might make
if it had passed harmlessly through and were flying away now,
on the far side, back into the realm of the imaginary.

Some with torn clothing, some bloodied,
some limping at top speed like children in a three-legged race,
some half dragged,
some intact in neat suits and dresses,
they walk in silence up the avenues,
all dusted to a ghostly whiteness,
all but their eyes, which are rubbed red as the eyes of a Zahoris,
who can see the dead under the ground.

Some died while calling home to say they were O.K.
Some died after over an hour spent learning they would die.
Some died so abruptly they may have seen death from within it.
Some broke windows and leaned out and waited for rescue.
Some were asphyxiated.
Some burned, their very faces caught fire.
Some fell, letting gravity speed them through their long
     moment.
Some leapt hand in hand, the elasticity in their last bits of love
     time letting—I wish I could say—their vertical streaks down
     the sky happen more lightly.

At the high window, where I've often stood
to escape a nightmare, I meet
the single, unblinking eye
that lights the all-night lifting
and sifting for bodies, for pieces of bodies,
for anything that is not nothing,
in the search that always goes on
somewhere, now in New York and Kabul.

On a street corner she holds up a picture—
of a man who is smiling. In the gray air
of today few pass. Sorry sorry sorry.
She startles. Suppose, down the street, that headlong lope . . .
Or over there, that hair so black it's purple . . .
And yet, suppose some evening I forgot
The fare and transfer, yet got by that way
Without recall,—lost yet poised in traffic.
Then I might find your eyes . . .

It could happen. Sorry sorry good luck thank you.
On this side it is "amnesia"—forgetting the way home—;
on the other, "invisibleness"—never entirely returning.
Hard to see clearly in the metallic mist,
or through the sheet of supposed reality
cast over our world, bourne that no creature born
pokes its way back through, and no love can tear.

The towers burn and fall, burn and fall—
in a distant shot, like smokestacks spewing oily earth remnants.
Schwarze Milch der Frühe wir trinken sie abends
wir trinken sie mittage und morgens wir trinken sie nachts
wir trinken und trinken
Here is not a comparison but a corollary,
not a likeness but a common lineage
in the twentieth-century history of violent death—
black men in the South castrated and hanged from trees,
soldiers advancing in mud at 90,000 dead per mile,
train upon train headed eastward of boxcars shoved full to the
        corners with Jews and Gypsies to be enslaved or gassed,
state murder of twenty, thirty, forty million of its own,
atomic blasts wiping cities off the earth, fire bombings the same,
death marches, starvations, assassinations, disappearances,
entire countries turned into rubble, minefields, mass graves.
Seeing the towers vomit these omens, that the last century
        dumped into this one, for us to dispose of, we know
they are our futures, that is our own black milk
        crossing the sky: *wir schaufeln ein Grab in den Lüften da*
        liegt man nicht eng

Burst jet fuel, incinerated aluminum, steel fume, volatized
        marble, exploded granite, pulverized wallboard, berserked
        plastic, mashed concrete, gasified mercury, scoria, vapor
of the vaporized—draped over our island up to streets regimented
        into numbers and letters,
breathed across the great bridges to Brooklyn and the waiting
        sea:
astringent, sticky, miasmic, empyreumatic,
air too foul to take in, but we take it in,

too gruesome for seekers of lost beloveds
to breathe, but they breathe it and you breathe it.

A photograph of a woman hangs
from his neck. He doesn't look up.
He stares down at the sidewalk of flagstone slabs
laid down in Whitman's century, gutter edges
iron wheels rasped long ago to a melted roundedness:
conscious mind envying the stones.
Nie stają się, są,
Nic nad to, myślalem,
zbrzydziwszy sobie
wszystko co staje się.

And I sat down by the waters of the Hudson,
by the North Cove Yacht Harbor, and thought
of what those on the high floors must have suffered: knowing
they would burn alive, and then, burning alive.
Could there be a mechanism of death
so mutilating to existence, that no one
gets over it ever, not even the dead?
And then I saw before me, in steel letters welded
to the steel railing posts, Walt Whitman's words
written when America plunged into war with itself:
City of the world! . . .
Proud and passionate city—mettlesome, mad, extravagant city!
Words of a time of illusions. And then I remembered
others of his words after the war was over and Lincoln dead:
I saw the debris and debris of all the slain soldiers of the war,
But I saw they were not as was thought,
They themselves were fully at rest—they suffer'd not,
The living remain'd and suffer'd, the mother suffer'd,
And the wife and the child and the musing comrade suffer'd . . .

In our minds the glassy blocks
succumb over and over into themselves,
slam down floor by floor into themselves.

They blow up as if in reverse, explode
downward and outward, billowing
through the streets, engulfing the fleeing.

Each tower as it falls concentrates
into itself, as if transforming itself
infinitely slowly into a black hole

infinitesimally small: mass
without space, where each light,
each life, put out, lies down within us.

from *The New Yorker*

After Horace

Ode 11, Book 12

◊　◊　◊

Spare me the Roman wars, and those
Who battled on in myth, when prose
Extends to suit these topics better
Than odes in their mellifluous meter.

Maecenas, think on this awhile:
Strong themes are suited to your style
Like dragging tyrants by their necks.
While my sweet Muse would sing of sex,

Of my fair lady, Licymnia
Who fondly hopes her heart will be a
Faithful devotee of mine
With eyes as shimmering as wine.

See how she glories at the chance
To show her prowess in the dance.
Though lightly clad, she's not the least
Shy of display at Diane's feast.

Tell me, Maecenas, wouldn't you
Abjure all wealth, and treasure too,
If Licymnia would choose to spare
One strand of her luxuriant hair?

Even if this flirtatious miss
Denies you the favor of one kiss
To disconcert you, makes you feel it,
She won't accept your kiss; she'll steal it!

from *Poetry*

Love Blooms at Chimsbury After the War

◇　◇　◇

After a round of croquet in the garden, Pimpton
dropped dead with our lunch in his hands. Then Babette
dropped dead under her wide brimmed straw hat. Poncey
dropped dead, then Alice, then Tuckles. The sweep dropped
dead from his perch on the roof, then Yappy, our cocker,
dropped dead under a bush. We peered out the gate, watched
the town dropping dead: the butcher all bloody, the bobby,
the old pony hitched to the dead iceman's ice cart
dropped dead. Then you dropped dead, sis, and I might've
too if not for a vision of young Harold Winter,
the vicar, drifting down on parachute strings,
"I fear it's all my fault," he laughs easily.
Our children take to the trees every summer
while swallows rain down like over-ripe plums.

from *Field*

Proverb

◇ ◇ ◇

Les morts vont vite, the dead go fast, the next day absent!
Et les vivants sont dingues, the living are haywire.
Except for a few who grieve, life rapidly readjusts itself
The milliner trims the hat not thinking of the departed
The horse sweats and throws his stubborn rider to the earth
Uncaring if he has killed him or not
The thrown man rises. But now he knows that he is not going,
Not going fast, though he was close to having been gone.
The day after Caesar's death, there was a new, bustling Rome
The moment after the racehorse's death, a new one is sought for
    the stable
The second after a moth's death there are one or two hundred other
    moths
The month after Einstein's death the earth is inundated with new
    theories
Biographies are written to cover up the speed with which we go:
No more presence in the bedroom or waiting in the hall
Greeting to say hello with mixed emotions. The dead go quickly
Not knowing why they go or where they go. To die is human,
To come back divine. Roosevelt gives way to Truman
Suddenly in the empty White House a brave new voice resounds
And the wheelchaired captain has crossed the great divide.
Faster than memories, faster than old mythologies, faster than the
    speediest train.
Alexander of Macedon, on time!
Prudhomme on time, Gorbachev on time, the beloved and the lover
    on time!

Les morts vont vite. We living stand at the gate
And life goes on.

from *The New York Review of Books*

Y2K (1933)

◊   ◊   ◊

The age demanded an image
Of its accelerated grimace
—Ezra Pound

Some of us were tempted to oblige,
Until the aesthetics got so complicated:
Private, yes, but at the same time
Sculpted as from stone and freighted with the
Weight and shape of history, each one
Part of something bigger, something
No one could explain, or even describe.
A *change* was on the way, eliding outwards
From the chambers of self-doubt into a torchlit Platz
In waves of imagery and rhetoric
That motioned towards some none too distant future
Where a narrow cage awaited, and Cassandra
Practiced the extreme, the fraudulent emotions.

So the image of the age wound down to insects in a jar:
The light flows in, and you can see for miles,
But try to move and something lifeless intervenes.
The truth is on the outside, where the atmosphere is far too
Rarified to breathe, while here inside the confines
Of our individual lives we reign as kings, as
Kings of the inconsequential. And the soul inscribes its
Shape in the profusion of the sky, yet its reality is
Small, and bounded on all sides
By language writhing with the unrequited

Ache of what was free and fine and
Now surrounds us everywhere, a medium
Too general to inhabit or feel.

"Look," I tell myself, I tell my soul,
"Those sentiments were fine, but they've had their say,
And something stronger is in the air, and you can feel it."
So the fantasy of now sustains an arc of flight
That takes it from a vague, malignant vacuum
To this calm suburban street where on a winter morning
Snow falls as the postman makes his rounds
And something gathers in the corners, something innocent
And evil as a sighing in the sky, insistent
And inert, dragged backwards by a constant
Nagging at the base of the brain, an ill-defined
Unease that hides the horror in the heart, but always working
Towards the future, towards the Führer.

from *Pleiades*

TED KOOSER

In the Hall of Bones

◇　◇　◇

Here we store the reassembled
scaffolding, the split, bleached uprights,
the knobby corner locks and braces
that held up the mastodon's
bag of wet leaves and the ivory
forklift of its head. Over there are
the planks upon which lay the turtle's
diving bell, and the articulated
rack that kept the dromedary's hump
from collapsing under the weight
of its perseverance. And here is
the basket that held the clip-clop
pulse of the miniature horse
as it dreamed of growing tall enough
to have lunch from a tree. And then
here's man, all matchsticks, wooden spoons
and tongue depressors wired together,
a rack supporting a leaky jug
of lust and worry. Of all the skeletons
assembled here, this is the only one
in which once throbbed a heart
made sad by brooding on its shadow.

from *Third Coast*

The Music of Time

◇ ◇ ◇

The young woman sewing
by the window hums a song
I don't know; I hear only
a few bars, and when the trucks
barrel down the broken street
the music is lost. Before the darkness
leaks from the shadows of
the great cathedral, I see her
once more at work and later
hear in the sudden silence
of nightfall wordless music rising
from her room. I put aside
my papers, wash, and dress
to eat at one of the seafood
places along the great avenues
near the port where later
the homeless will sleep. Then I
I walk for hours in the Barrio
Chino passing the open
doors of tiny bars and caves
from which the voices of old men
bark out the stale anthems
of love's defeat. "This is the world,"
I think, "this is what I came
in search of years ago." Now I
can go back to my single room,
I can lie awake in the dark
rehearsing all the trivial events
of the day ahead, a day that begins

when the sun clears the dark spires
of someone's God, and I waken
in a flood of dust rising from
nowhere and from nowhere comes
the actual voice of someone else.

from *Rattle*

Jihad

◇   ◇   ◇

A contrail's white scimitar unsheathes
Above the tufts of anti-aircraft fire.
Before the mullah's drill on righteousness,
Practice rocks are hurled at chicken-wire

Dummies of tanks with silhouetted infidels
Defending the nothing both sides fight over
In God's name, a last idolatry
Of boundaries. The sirens sound: take cover.

He has forced the night and day, the sun and moon,
Into your service. By His leave, the stars
Will shine to light the path that He has set

You to walk upon. His mercy will let
You slay who would blaspheme or from afar
Defile His lands. Glory is yours, oh soon.

Of the heart. Of the tongue. Of the sword. The holy war
Is waged against the self at first, to raze
The ziggurat of sin we climb upon
To view ourselves, and next against that glaze

The enemies of faith will use to disguise
Their words. Only then, and at the caliph's nod,
Are believers called to drown in blood the people
Of an earlier book. There is no god but God.

He knows the day of death and sees how men
Will hide. Who breaks His covenant is cursed.
Who slights His revelations will live in fire.

He has cast aside the schemer and the liar
Who mistake their emptiness of heart for a thirst
That, to slake, the streams of justice descend.

Ski-masked on videotape, the skinny martyr
Reads his manifesto. He's stilted, nervous.
An hour later, he's dropped at the market town,
Pays his fare, and climbs aboard the bus.

Strapped to his chest is the death of thirty-four
—Plus his own—"civilians" on their way
To buy or sell what goods they claim are theirs,
Unlike our fates, which are not ours to say.

Under the shade of swords lies paradise.
Whom you love are saved with you, their souls
In His hand. And who would want to return to life

Except to be killed again? Who can thrive
On the poverty of this world, its husks and holes?
His wisdom watches for each sacrifice.

from *Poetry*

To Zbigniew Herbert's Bicycle

◇ ◇ ◇

Since he never
really possessed you
however he may have longed to
in secret

so that in dreams he knew
each surface and detail of you
gleam of spokes and chrome
smells of grease and rubber
the chain's black knuckles

day by day you
remained out of sight
so that he never had to
lock you up or hide you
because nobody could see you

and though he never
in fact learned how to ride you
keeping his round
toppling weight upright
on the two small toes
of water slipping
out from under

once he was well away
hands on the grips feet off the ground
you could take him
anywhere

at last like the rain
through the rain

invisible as you were

from *The New Yorker*

Dear Alter Ego

◇ ◇ ◇

I wish to cancel my subscription to your
deviance, the dither of which could send me
to cloister oneself in darkest Moorhead,
or maybe prison—just far away from you
and the Book of Books discussion group on Tuesdays.
I built a maquette of a johnboat, see,
and soon as I can light this match, the prayer
is cast for ferrymen or Noah's shining legacy
to appear with a Thermos™ full
of bourbon and a chart to pirate me away.
Locked in the trunk of your three-tone sedan
You'll find those grafts and gifts you wouldn't share—
The loopworm embedded in glassy lava,
the bulb syringe, the yokes,
the black-light poster of your messianic
desires, and one splintered dowsing rod.

from *Croonenbergh's Fly*

A History of Color

◊ ◊ ◊

1.

What is heaven but the history of color,
dyes washed out of laundry, cloth and cloud,
mystical rouge, lipstick, eye shadows? Harlot nature,
explain the color of tongue, lips, nipples,
against Death come ons of labia, penis, the anus,
the concupiscent color wheels of insects and birds,
explain why Christian gold and blue tempt the kneeling,
why Moslem green is miraculous in the desert,
why the personification of the rainbow is Iris,
the mother of Eros, why *Adam* in Hebrew
comes out of the redness of earth . . .
The cosmos and impatiens I planted this June
may outlast me, these yellow, pink and blue annuals
do not sell indulgences, a rose ravishes a rose.
The silver and purple pollen that has blown on the roof
of my car concludes a sacred conversation.

Against Death washerwomen and philosophers
sought a fixative for colors to replace unstable substances
like saliva, urine, and blood, the long process of boiling,
washing, and rinsing. It is Death who works
with clean hands and a pure heart. Against him
Phoenician red-purple dyes taken from sea snails, the colors
fixed by exposing wool to air of the morning seas near Sidon,
or the sunlight and winds on the limestone cliffs of Crete—
all lost, which explains a limestone coastline
changed into mountains of pink-veined marble,

the discarded bodies of gods.
Of course Phoenician purple made for gods
and heroes cannot be produced nowadays.
Virgil thought purple was the color of the soul—
all lost. Anyone can see the arithmetic when purple
was pegged to the quantity and price of seashells.

Remember
the common gray and white seagull looked down
at the Roman Republic, at the brick-red and terra-cotta
dominant after the pale yellow stone of the Greek world,
into the glare of the Empire's white marble.
The sapphire and onyx housefly that circled
the jeweled crowns of Byzantium buzzed prayers,
thinks what it thinks, survives. Under a Greek sky
the churches held Christ alive to supplicants,
a dove alighted on a hand torn by nails.
In holy light and darkness
the presence of Christ is cupped in silver.
Death holds, whether you believe Christ
is there before you or not, you will not see Him later—
sooner prick the night sky with a needle to find the moon.

2.

I fight Death with peppermints, a sweet to recall
the Dark Ages before the word *orange* existed.
In illuminated manuscripts St. Jerome,
his robes *egg-red,* is seen translating in the desert,
a golden lion at his feet—
or he is tied to a column naked in a dream,
flagellated for reading satires and Pliny's
Natural History that describes
the colors used by Apelles, the Greek master,
in a painting of grapes so true to life
birds would alight on them to feed.
Death, you tourist, you've seen it all and better before,
your taste: whipped saints sucking chastity's thumb,
while you eat your candy of diseased and undernourished infants.

On an afternoon when Death seemed no more than a newspaper
in a language I could not read, I remember
looking down at Jerusalem from the Mount of Olives,
that my friend said: "Jerusalem is a harlot,
everyone who passes leaves a gift."
Do birds of prey sing madrigals?
Outside the walls of Jerusalem, the crusaders
dumped mounts of dead Muslims
and their green banners, the severed heads of Jews,
some still wrapped in prayer-shawls,
while the Christian dead sprawled near the place of a skull
which is called in Hebrew *Golgotha*.
Among the living, blood and blood-soaked prayers,
on the land of God's broken promises—a flagged javelin
stuck into the Holy Sepulcher as into a wild boar.

Hauled back by the *Franks,* colors never seen in Europe,
wonders of Islam, taffetas, organdies, brocades, damasks.
Gold-threaded cloth that seemed made for the Queen of Heaven
was copied in Italy on certain paintings of Our Lady,
on her blue robes in gold in Arabic:
There is no God but God, Muhammad is His Prophet—
for whom but Death to read.
Wrapped in a looted prayer rug,
an idea seized by Aquinas: the separation of faith and reason.
Later nicked from the library of Baghdad:
the invention of paper brought from China
by pilgrims on a hajj, looted rhyme, lenses,
notes on removing cataracts.
Certain veils would be lifted from the eyes of Europe,
all only for Death to see.

Within sight of Giotto's white, green and pink marble bell-tower
that sounded the promise of Paradise,
plants and insects were used for dyes made from oak gall,
bastard saffron, beetle, canary weed, cockroach,
the fixative was fermented piss from a young boy
or a man drunk on red wine, while the painters
mixed their pigments with egg yolks and albumen,
gold with lime, garlic, wax, and casein

that dried hard as adamantine, buffed with a polished agate
or a wolf's tooth.

At the time of the Plague, while the dead
lay unattended in the streets of Europe,
the yellow flag hung out more often than washing,
someone cloistered wrote a text
on making red from cinnabar, saffron from crocus,
each page an illuminated example.
At the Last Supper the disciples sat dead at table.
Still, by the late fifteenth century
color was seen as ornament,
almost parallel to the colors of rhetoric,
blue was moving away from its place describing
the vaults of heaven to the changing sky of everyday.
Does it matter to heaven if a sleeve is blue or red or black?
In Venice Titian found adding lead-white to azurite-blue
changed a blue sleeve to satin.

3.

I think the absence of color is like a life without love.
A master can draw every passion with a pencil, but light,
shadow and dark cannot reveal the lavender Iris
between the opened thighs of a girl still almost a child,
or before life was through with her, the red and purple
pomegranate at the center of her being.

Against Death on an English day Newton discovered
a single ray of white light refracted,
decomposed into a spectrum of colors,
that he could reconstruct the totality,
mischievously reverse the process
and produce white light again—which perhaps is why
last century, in a painting by Max Ernst,
the Holy Mother is spanking the baby Jesus.

Goethe found a like proof on a sunny summer day—
the birds, I suppose, as usual devouring insects

courting to the last moment of life.
While sitting by a crystal pool watching
soldiers fishing for trout, the poet was taken
by spectrums of color refracted from a ceramic shard
at the bottom of the pool, then from the tails of swimming trout
catching fire and disappearing,
until a rush of thirsty horses, tired and dirtied by war,
muddied the waters.

A heroic tenor sings to the exploding sun:
every war is a new dawning—Fascist music.
Death would etch Saturn devouring his children on coins,
if someone would take his money.
Of course his I O U is good as gold.

Turner had sailors lash him to the mast
to see into a storm, then he painted slavers
throwing overboard the dead and dying,
sharks swimming through shades of red—
lashed to the mast, as Odysseus had himself lashed
not to hear the sirens sing how he would be remembered.
Later he painted the atheist Avalanche, then heaven
in truthful colors: Rain, Steam, Speed.
Portraits of nothing and very like, they said, *tinted steam.*
Turner kept most of his paintings to leave to England,
his Burning of the Houses of Parliament.

Against oblivion a still life of two red apples
stands for a beautiful woman. On her shoulder
the bruise of a painter's brush—she is no more
than a still life of peasant shoes.
You will not keep apples or shoes or France, Death says.
A child chooses an object first for color,
then for form, in rooms with mother, father,
Death, and all the relatives of being.

4.

Now this coloratura moves off-stage
to the present, which is a kind of intermission.
My friend Mark Rothko painted a last canvas,
gray and yellow, then took a kitchen knife, half cut off his wrists
bound and knotted behind his back,
(a trick of the mind Houdini never mastered),
to throw off Eros, who rode his back and whipped him
even after he was dead, till Eros, the little Greek,
was covered with blood of the Song of Songs.
Now Rothko is a study of color, a purple chapel,
a still river where he looks for his mother and father.

Death, you tourist with too much luggage,
you can distinguish the living from your dead.
Can you tell Poseidon's trident from a cake fork,
the living from the living,
winter from summer, autumn from spring?
In a sunless world, even bats nurse their young,
hang upside down looking for heaven,
make love in a world where the lion, afraid of no beast,
runs in terror from a white chicken. Such are your winnings.
Death, I think you take your greatest pleasure
in watching us murdering in great numbers
in ways even you have not planned.
They say in paradise every third thought is of earth
and a woman with a child at her breast.

from *American Poetry Review*

PAUL MULDOON

The Loaf

◇   ◇   ◇

When I put my finger to the hole they've cut for a dimmer switch
in a wall of plaster stiffened with horsehair
it seems I've scratched a two-hundred-year-old itch

with a pink and a pink and a pinkie-pick.

When I put my ear to the hole I'm suddenly aware
of spades and shovels turning up the gain
all the way from Raritan to the Delaware

with a clink and a clink and a clinky-click

When I put my nose to the hole I smell the flood-plain
of the canal after a hurricane
and the spots of green grass where thousands of Irish have lain

with a stink and a stink and a stinky-stick.

When I put my eye to the hole I see one holding horsedung to the
        rain
in the hope, indeed, indeed,
of washing out a few whole ears of grain

with a wink and a wink and a winkie-wick

And when I do at last succeed
on putting my mouth to the horsehair-fringed niche
I can taste the small loaf of bread he baked from that whole seed

with a link and a link and a linky-lick.

from *The New York Review of Books*

Four Deaths
That Happened Daily

◇   ◇   ◇

1.

One day I died while preparing to live.
The killer stepped out of a Seurat painting
And said, "I will make you into a million dots,
Watch your blood divide on divided sidewalks,
Stipple blackened sheets with holes to become stars.
I will wax messianic while holding your implosion
In a glass of Kool Aid." He pressed me
Up against the plastered canvas
And then I felt the holes bore through me
And saw the Rorschach he had made,
His little gory Freud. At last,
I thought as I gazed at the stars
On my chest. The light.

2.

It happens in the frilled distillery of our love, in the bleak distance
        to lights like warm cheeks
And streets that smell like seals and clatter at the end like wartime
        reels, and we die
While we wait for the abolitionists of chiaroscuro. And once the
        glib propaganda spills its

Cellophane, there are numbers like racing hands and then white.
　　　The clatter sounds
Like a little Swastika. The darkness coughs. And dear God, why
　　　doesn't it end?

3.

Where the Apartheid of an eyelash gashes the sky
Make a wish, child.
Make a wish upon your bullet hole, and watch your mother
Shrink into the small old doll
You thought she'd never be. Remember biblically:
Woman came from the erosion of bone.
So when you blink yourself to sleep
Seductive sickles mar your dreams.
Look: there is the reaper, he is guarding your sweet eyes.

4.

Up and down Hope Street
Children outgrew their underwear
And death escaped from its zoos.
My motor ran on, elegiac
And I saw the red light but disobeyed it
Because I wanted to be dead
But felt remarkably good,
Better than I'd felt in months.
I left my blood in its jar of protest,
To die color blind, to invert Christmas,
I didn't care whose hell it was.
The police came to question me
So I would envy the wild horses in their guns.

from *Spoon River Poetry Review*

MARILYN NELSON

Asparagus

◇ ◇ ◇

He taught me how to slurp asparagus:
You hold it in your fingers, eat the stem
by inches to the tender terminus,
then close your eyes and suck in the sweet gem.
First, cook it in its own delicious steam,
sauté breadcrumbs in butter separately,
combine, eat slowly. As he ate, a gleam
in his eyes twinkled with such *jeu d'esprit,*
it made me drunk with longing. In my chair
amid our laughing, slurping dinner guests,
I felt as smug as a new billionaire,
not jealous, not rejected, not depressed,
as almost obscene, almost a debauché,
he slurped asparagus, and winked at me.

from *Rattapallax*

DANIEL NESTER

Poem for the Novelist Whom I Forced to Write a Poem

◇ ◇ ◇

You left before I could say you didn't have to do it!
Instead, you mailed me this wonderful hybrid,
this laundry list you never see anywhere anymore.
To put it simply: I cried. We poets always leave those
    things out
and focus on the birds at the feeder, as if they could tell us
anything, ever. You told me you watch boxing. When I said
you were as old as my mother, I didn't mean to make you
feel old or try to make you my mother. I was trying
to give you details. But now I read that you believe in
    God
and so do I, and I've got to thinking maybe
there's a novel in me yet! Then I look on my desk, the
    obese orange
left over from lunch, and I'm reminded why
Frank O'Hara said he didn't paint. He hated the details.
But I think you are a poet, Christina, a Greek goddess
descended from Cavafy who, like me, tries to get
all the details down. So when you go back to that novel
of the child in Japan searching for the clear magic stone,
remember the cold afternoon you sang a different tune
and switched teams. We'll miss you over here.
We need people like you. Mix up your punches, and
remember the neverending lists, the long, otherworldly
    story.

from *Spinning Jenny*

What Happened to Everybody

◊ ◊ ◊

Lodholz, Schwendener, Bauer, Kraft. The one who was thin got fat & the one who was fat, athletic. So many Chinese restaurants! Now there is a walking tour. Historical buildings. Douglas went into oil. He moved to Houston & his parents do not remember me though their son has appeared in more than one of my writings. They don't look happy to hear this. *By name?* they say. *You said his name?* Schoolyard swoon: 120 years of echoing kids. I find my spot behind a tree. In a trashcan, "My Personal Dictionary" hand-lettered by Eric. Open to L: *Look, Love, Live, Lose, Listen, Light.* Everything he needed right there on one page—how could he throw it away? My friend Marcia lives in her parents' house. Show me the laundry chute. The bulletin board. The room where we played Parcheesi with our brothers on a low coffee table while our parents discussed business in the living room. The Canadians split up. The Italians moved west. Many people disappeared entirely though their porch steps retain the same chips & cracks. *Here is the ditch where I lost my blue sewing thread. The house we were scared of. The auto body shop. The grocery store where my brother dropped a watermelon so they would give it to us free.* Missy & her father put Missy's mother into a nursing home (*she wasn't even sick*) then flew off to Europe. They sent postcards back to the neighbors, who never mentioned when they visited Missy's mother what a great time Missy & her dad were having. *She could have gone too. Why would you do that to your own mother?* Missy came home to plan her wedding & Missy's father went on to Cairo to see the pyramids, his biggest dream. *He fell over dead at the foot of the Sphinx.* Sent home in a coffin, the neighbors swear he looked positively Egyptian.

from *LUNA*

137

Queen Min Bi

◇   ◇   ◇

Queen Min was the bomb. Smooth forehead, perfectly
parted thick hair, and plum lips at fourteen
enough to make any pedophile happy.
So the king handpicked her,

orphan Korean girl born in Yuhju, stringless,
to be a royal marionette—who would have guessed
she owned a wooden heart to match any politician's?

Maybe she abused her handservants.
Maybe she pumped into her husband
doggy style with an early bamboo Korean
strap-on and that's why she never had children.

Maybe that made Hwang so happy even after
she died, throat sliced open by invading Japanese,
he carved her name into a slab of man-sized marble
by hand, honoring a woman who snatched his kingdom

without a glance back at history,
what those scrolls dictated for female behavior.
I want to be like her, befriending pale-
skinned foreigners and infuriating her father-in-law

enough for him to conspire toward her death
while commoners rested head to stone pillow
and dreamt of her brow-raising power;
16 when she married, 32 when she died—

before Japanese flags cloaked our country,
before Korean housewives lay beaten
without domestic violence laws to halfway shield
their swollen faces. Half a world away

nisei Korean children flinch at the smack of skin
on skin, memorize the hiss of curses like bullets,
and I wish she were more than dust and legend,
more than a sold-out opera at Lincoln Center

or part of a wistful poem; I want to inherit
that tiger part of her, the part that got her killed,
the part that inflamed my eyes and had me tracing the
clay walls of her birthplace with fingers in the rain, wanting

to collect and construct a woman out of myth.
So by Chinese calendar she's a rabbit, her favorite
drink was macculi, the moonshine of Korea, her
left breast slightly heavier than her right

and maybe she kissed her husband Hwang
on the forehead before overtaking his kingdom,
as Queen Min Bi, so loved by all they called her Mama.

from *Barrow Street*

Anniversary

◇   ◇   ◇

September 2002

We adore images, we like the spectacle
Of speed and size, the working of prodigious
Systems. So on television we watched

The terrible spectacle, repetitiously gazing
Until we were sick not only of the sight
Of our prodigious systems turned against us

But of the very systems of our watching.
The date became a word, an anniversary
That we inscribed with meanings—who keep so few,

More likely to name an airport for an actor
Or athlete than "First of May" or "Fourth of July."
In the movies we dream up, our captured heroes

Tell the interrogator their commanding officer's name
Is Colonel Donald Duck—he writes it down, code
Of a lowbrow memory so assured it's nearly

Aristocratic. Some say the doomed firefighters
Before they hurried into the doomed towers wrote
Their Social Security numbers on their forearms.

Easy to imagine them kidding about it a little,
As if they were filling out some workday form.
Will Rogers was a Cherokee, a survivor

Of expropriation. A roper, a card. For some,
A hero. He had turned sixteen the year
That Frederick Douglass died. Douglass was twelve

When Emily Dickinson was born. Is even Donald
Half-forgotten?—Who are the Americans, not
A people by blood or religion? As it turned out,

The donated blood not needed, except as meaning.
And on the other side that morning the guy
Who shaved off all his body hair and screamed

The name of God with his boxcutter in his hand.
O Americans—as Marianne Moore would say,
Whence is our courage? Is what holds us together

A gluttonous dreamy thriving? Whence our being?
In the dark roots of our music, impudent and profound?—
Or in the Eighteenth Century clarities

And mystic Masonic totems of the Founders:
The Eye of the Pyramid watching over us,
Hexagram of Stars protecting the Eagle's head

From terror of pox, from plague and radiation.
And if they blow up the Statue of Liberty—
Then the survivors might likely in grief, terror

And excess build a dozen more, or produce
A catchy song about it, its meaning as beyond
Meaning as those symbols, or Ray Charles singing "America

The Beautiful." Alabaster cities, amber waves,
Purple majesty. The back-up singers in sequins
And high heels for a performance—or in the studio

In sneakers and headphones, engineers at soundboards,
Musicians, all concentrating, faces as grave
With purpose as the harbor Statue herself.

from *The Washington Post Magazine*

What the Paymaster Said

◇ ◇ ◇

Instead of a paycheck, the company offered me kind thoughts. *We'll give you three,* the paymaster said, *one for your diligence and two for your beautiful wife.* No, no. I did not want their kind thoughts. I'd had enough of them.

If not that, the paymaster said, *then what about apples? They are delicious apples, fresh from Wisconsin, and sweet. Under every one, the fruitpicker has held his palm, has wobbled each apple until it fell ripely into his hand of its own accord. Three bushels.* But I did not want their apples. I wanted what was mine.

We must learn not to be selfish in difficult times, the paymaster said, *but you type quite well. You type superbly, your fingers flashing across the keyboard like beautiful blades of tall grass when the wind blows from the distant mountains. I will give you cigarettes for your typing, or I will give you bombs.*

The bombs are quite nice. They fall from airplanes which you will rent by the hour. The company will lease you an airplane at a discounted rate, but the bombs will be yours to keep. You have such a pleasant manner, we can't afford to lose you. So I make this fine offer. I shook my head. I didn't want cigarettes or bombs. I have many mouths to feed, and my wife would not be happy if I brought home only bombs.

The paymaster sighed and adjusted his coat so the gold buttons winked in the office lights. *You are ungrateful,* he told me, *but I will offer you one more thing. Instead of a paycheck, I will give you coffins. The grain is as fine as a dragonfly's wing. Coffins for your entire family—all at the company's generous expense.*

from *Witness*

Sequoia sempervirens

◇　◇　◇

We are about what　　a squirrel's size
is to a tree　　to this tree

we are the miles as shoe to
city limits　　one line

we rip around
getting our nut

off　　to the city;

foot totals map　　layered upward
impossible city on top of city

even down　　underground
into time

it seems to

have grown from our gotten
nut　　the fruits of a pleasure

in lifting our scale into the scale
of a weight we feel　　we're part of

into this other dish we can feel
rest into balance

our nature in nature
nature   in us

The long stabilized climate   the fattening

of an abundant season
the people pack on

into a city:
venerable aging of the gather

into the fold's royal robe   venerable aging
of the met crowd into community;

the self destructions squirreled away in what grows

Settled.

But we seem almost a fire dependent
species like this tree

one that grows around fire
as if burn   were a wire fence a post

of imbedded iron   a piece of shot
a plate in our heads

for the guest lightning.

from *Callaloo*

The Disappearances

◊ ◊ ◊

"Where was it one first heard of the truth?"

On a day like any other day,
like "yesterday or centuries before,"
in a town with the one remembered street,
shaded by the buckeye and the sycamore—
the street long and true as a theorem,
the day like yesterday or the day before,
the street you walked down centuries before—
the story the same as the others flooding in
from the cardinal points is
turning to take a good look at you.
Every creature, intelligent or not, has disappeared—
the humans, phosphorescent,
the duplicating pets, the guppies and spaniels,
the Woolworth's turtle that cost forty-nine cents
(with the soiled price tag half-peeled on its shell)—
but from the look of things, it only just happened.
The wheels of the upside-down tricycle are spinning.
The swings are empty but swinging.
And the shadow is still there, and there
is the object that made it,
riding the proximate atmosphere,
oblong and illustrious above
the dispeopled bedroom community,
venting the memories of those it took,
their corrosive human element.
This is what you have to walk through to escape,
transparent but alive as coal dust.

This is what you have to hack through,
bamboo-tough and thickly clustered.
The myths are somewhere else, but here are the meanings,
and you have to breathe them in
until they burn your throat
and peck at your brain with their intoxicated teeth.
This is you as seen by them, from the corner of an eye
(was that the way you were always seen?).
This is you when the president died
(the day is brilliant and cold).
This is you poking a ground-wasps' nest.
This is you at the doorway, unobserved,
while your aunts and uncles keen over the body.
This is your first river, your first planetarium, your first Popsicle.
The cold and brilliant day in six-color prints—
but the people on the screen are black and white.
Your friend's mother is saying,
Hush, children! Don't you understand history is being made?
You do, and you still do. Made and made again.
This is you as seen by them, and them as seen by you,
and you as seen by you, in five dimensions,
in seven, in three again, then two,
then reduced to a dimensionless point
in a universe where the only constant is the speed of light.
This is you at the speed of light.

from *The New Yorker*

Sleet

◊ ◊ ◊

What was it like before the doctor got there?

Till then, we were in the back seat of the warm
dark bubble of the old Buick. We were where
we'd never not been, no matter where we were.

And when the doctor got there?

Everything outside was in a rage of wind and sleet,
we were children, brothers, safe in the back seat,
for once not fighting, just listening, watching the storm.

Weren't you afraid that something bad might happen?

Our father held the wheel with just two fingers,
even though the car skidded and fishtailed,
and the chains clanged raggedly over ice and asphalt.

Weren't you afraid at all?

Dad sang for someone to fly him to the moon,
to let him play among the stars, while mom
held up the lighter to another Marlboro.

But when the doctor started speaking . . .

The tip of the Marlboro was a bright red star.
Her lips pursed and she released the ring of Saturn,
which dissolved as we caught at it, as my dad sang Mars.

When you realized what the doctor was saying . . .

They were closer to the storm in the front seat.
The high beams were weak as steam against the walled swirling,
only illuminated what we couldn't see.

When he described it, the tumor in his brain and what it meant . . .

See, we were children. Then we weren't. Or my brother wasn't.
He was driving now, he gripped the steering wheel
with both hands, and stared hard at the panicked wipers.

What did you feel?

Just sleet, the slick road, the car going way too fast,
no brother beside me in the back seat, no singing father,
no mother, no ring of Saturn to catch as it floats.

from *Third Coast*

For Nazim Hikmet in the Old Prison, Now a Four Seasons Hotel

◇　◇　◇

It was from your prison I woke
to the muezzin calling at dawn.
From unbarred windows I saw
six minarets in a brightening sky,
the crescent moon beside Sophia
still there, absolutely
clear in March, the month
my mother always dies,
and I was rising
from fresh sheets to apricots and figs
delivered to our door.
It was your prison
and I couldn't change that.
My bed didn't spring with bugs,
I didn't wait for water
to thaw in the earthen jug,
it ran warm or cold
as I desired. To my touch.
I held your words next to me

. . . live with the outside,
with its people and animals, struggle and wind—
*   I mean with the outside beyond the walls.*

I mean however and wherever we are,
we must live as if we will never die

and when the day came
I walked out into the courtyard
flooded with sun
onto the old street, and I could turn
right or left. I couldn't help it—
walking on your footprints.

from *Rattapallax*

BRUCE SMITH

Song with a Child's Pacifier in It

◇ ◇ ◇

Indolent days in exile from Alabama in a city
    My city was a school
in the north I was bussed into: *I don't hate it I don't hate it*
    cinderblocks of kismet and John Wayne, I do
I don't, where the streets around the sublet are cordoned off
    black like a white kid in detention
for excavating graves of pre-war water and utopian electric
    erotic possibilities of wrongness like a guitar I plucked
threads from the millrace and the loom. When the hot-patch
    hot flash, all adrenaline and vibration, b-twang squeak, semi
truck backs up it makes the sound of an ambulance in France
    conscious of a language of hurt in sweet, predestined ways
and the air is perfumed with the lacquered black oil spilled
    and volition like a little philosopher of hell, I argued
at a great distance from Arabia and Pec, then mopped up and
    to myself said scat and blasphemous prayers
tamped in a form of a coffin. A fine film over the new
    The city was a film of another world inside this one
a planetary dust over the remains: an imitation pearl
    glaze over the beads of the glorified
plastic tiara, a winged copy of *Spare Change* in the gutter, an oven mitt
    an oven, an ocean passage, a lost nation
a child's pacifier, a lipstick casing, a pencil
    can you remember this? Akhmatova was asked
but who would write except the indolent? The air
    I remember the air in summer was an atom flow

rarefied with transmissions over the hidden speakers for Cubanismo
      karmic missiles and John Wayne marines and a boy
who will play a benefit for *la causa*. It's all in the rib cage
      It's all in the belly button, the coach says
A partially repatriated émigré with a crushed hat, I carry
      the outside boy of body, the inside boy of mind
in a wheelbarrow my heterosexual agenda: difference
      that schizophrenia I will carry to the flame and ash
(and shame and shamelessness). I return to the smoke of time
      In the city I fell in love
in Boston when I loved the numinous
      with Mistress Errato and the difference and the evening light
and now I await the dream trials
      for the crimes of 1965, your honor
where exhibit A is rhythm and blues, exhibit B a curl of hair
      I accuse myself of wanting a life
wrapped around a finger then unwound stretched from the
      willful and fatal, enraged and tender, the lifelong split
the Balkans through policy through rapture of the past
      of the self: in the American tar and becoming uneasy
to Tuscaloosa where I will delay the verdict with a song

from *Boston Review*

There's Trouble Everywhere

◊   ◊   ◊

There the blind man and his personal dark,
dawn like an emission between buildings,
arrested in the street a second,
meline, no, saffron, a peckish, dilute yellow
and uncontrollable like the light in
a Lorrain painting,
the dawn bearing down out
of its momentary stall,
there the blind man avec dog,
a man who can't suddenly dash
across the street crying *Martha, is it you,*
but must wait
for the dog's slow mind to consider
the next step. And those black wings leaving the scene,
the creases of analgetic green in the young trees
like the heaviness in the shoulders
after adolescence, the
description of life's deeper meaning
in the curve of the homeless man's body, asleep
on his sweater, the young woman walking fast
who looks as if small bits of veneer
have been chipped away, these
speak of something important just arriving.
An old obsession's slowly dying. The day
refers to itself in the third person, like the grinning maniac
who greets you as if he knows you. It's always
morning somewhere, you think,
but this doesn't have any hold on you now.
Even as you move you are reaching back

for something, some lien on existence
you remember, some slab or kitchen step you sat on
listening to the interior noises, the rhythm—you
say to yourself now—of a continuity
you haven't been able to find since,
but it isn't that easy, and it never was.
Always some criminal loose on the property,
moving closer. Some name you
once went by
inscribed inside the wedding band
of an unidentified corpse pulled from the river.
And the love you were so sure of,
that appears like a shape in the trees
on a leeward reach, the vast greenery
uprooted from some rain forest empire,
squeaks and trembles, or this
is only the blur cornering on Tenth.
Whatever might change what's wrong
won't declare itself. And the young poet,
an austere woman briskly climbing
the stairs at the cineplex, looks
haggard and close to despair,
but says nothing as you pass; it's not necessary
at this time to beg rescue, not yet,
though summer's heavy on the town,
and the well-watered lawn
by the cathedral's not open to our citizens.

from *Poetry*

Translating

◇　◇　◇

What are the characters eating in this novel
published in Barcelona in 1901
that I found this summer in my rented house?
It's raining hard. I've nothing else to read,
so I'm struggling with my high school Spanish.
What's *gragea*? *Cassell's Spanish Dictionary*
tells me it's a small, colored *bonbon,*
but, couched in odd British English,
other words make no sense. Two characters
walk through a plantation of *guindo* trees,
but when I look up the word, I see it means
mazzard in English. I read another page
almost understanding the stiff dialogue
until one character starts talking about
humazga, translated as *hearth-money,* or *fumage*—
what's that? An offering to the gods,
or the cost of fuel? *Cassell's* falls open
on my lap, and my eye skims down the columns
discovering that we lack words in English for
all kinds of stuff that happens every day,
the act of doffing the hat, hunting with ferrets,
and the prick of stubble in a horse's eye,
that there are many things we've never named
properly, like tubes for sampling sherry,
large bushy wigs, cakes kneaded with oil,
deadly carrots, and large, uneven teeth.
I close the book, then notice a little *salton,*
or *grasshopper,* clinging to the window ledge,
his hind legs folded, waiting for the sun

just like me. I look up *boredom.*
Why, the word doesn't exist.
And, really, why would anyone wish for it
when there's *borecale* and *boree,* English words
I've never even heard of before, but defined
in Spanish, one a *cabbage,* the other a *dance.*

from *Mid-American Review* and *Poetry Daily*

Lines

◇ ◇ ◇

Voice, perhaps you are the universe,
the hum of spiders.
If on the mountain a single bear
comes into the orchard;
much less, the husk of a locust
drops from the currant bush;
or the wind rattles a loose clapboard,
exchanging one skin for another—
it is the self longing to cross the barrier.
Sensing the visitors who hide among us,
the air enters and takes away.
Sharp as the odor of fresh sawdust,
the color of lost rooms,
those erotic odors, angst of brevity;
like crossing your thighs
in a spasm of loneliness.

from *PMS*

The Restaurant Business

◇   ◇   ◇

Elsie and I were having a nice, little romantic
dinner at our favorite restaurant, when the owner of
the restaurant came over and sat down at our table.
We had always greeted one another in a friendly fashion,
but we had never had an actual conversation with him
before. "I have no life," he said. "I work nineteen
hours a day. I employ a hundred-and-twenty people.
There's more paper work than you could ever imagine.
This place is killing me," he said with tears in his
eyes. We had stopped eating and just stared at him
in dumbfoundment. "Everybody needs a life," I said.
"You could sell the place." "My customers would kill
me. I have customers who drive two-hundred-and-fifty
miles each week to eat here. What would I tell them?"
he said. "You could change your name and move far
away, live in the wilderness with lots of animals,"
I said. Our food was getting cold. Neither of us
had taken a bite since he joined us. "But my guilt,
I'd have to live with a terrible guilt. The thought
of taking away so much pleasure from so many fine
people would keep me from enjoying anything," he said.
"But you said that you have no life, didn't you?"
Elsie said. There was a note of exasperation in her
voice. "My wife would have left me long ago if it
weren't for the money. She's the one that gets to
enjoy that, I don't," he said. It's true, the place
was always packed. He was making a ton of money.
"I don't get to do anything. My children grew up
without me. I own a boat, but I've only been on it

once. I don't go to movies, I don't watch television. I don't know anything about sports or politics. It's a pathetic way to live," he said. I looked at Elsie. She looked like she wanted to slap him, and not just once. "I had always thought you were really something. Boy, was I mistaken. Everybody has a life, everybody but you. And what right do you think you have to spoil our romantic meal with your contemptible story?" I said. "In here, I'm God. This is my kingdom, and you are my peasant serfs. You eat only what I'm willing to give you. And when I talk, you must listen. Scum," he said, and walked off, erect, chest pushed out, proud, possessed.

from *New American Writing*

The Lost Boy

◇　◇　◇

Across the Poudre river bridge
stands a stone monument to a lost boy.
Carved words fix the mystery. Did
he wander off, or was he carried off
by tooth or talon? Family, friends,
searched the mountainside calling his
name. The weather turned. Sleet, wind,
snow in slants across the ponderosas.
He blacked out under the canyon's
Milky Way. I hear his cries in
echoing arroyos. Though his bones
mouldered in cold drizzle he comes
crashing through wild plum thickets
clutching at my shirt, asking where I was
in his sagebrush hours. Through his
ripped jacket a flash of bone. I dare not
touch his skeletal shoulder. He's forgotten
how to be alive. The climb is no relief,
his weight dogs my knees. Breezes
sough through purple yarrow aspen groves,
dry waterfalls. I reach the cloud meadows,
hairpin switchbacks until Mount
Greyrock juts its granite forehead into
one hard thought: what remains unfinished
in the soul keeps doubling back
until earth and sky are balanced aches
like the cliff swallow's swift flight.

from *LUNA*

161

After Your Death

◇ ◇ ◇

First, I emptied the closets of your clothes,
threw out the bowl of fruit, bruised
from your touch, left empty the jars

you bought for preserves. The next morning,
birds rustled the fruit trees, and later
when I twisted a ripe fig loose from its stem,

I found it half-eaten, the other side
already rotting, or—like another I plucked
and split open—being taken from the inside:

a swarm of insects hollowing it. I'm too late,
again, another space emptied by loss.
Tomorrow, the bowl I have yet to fill.

from *New England Review*

On Being Asked to Discuss Poetic Theory

◇   ◇   ◇

I know for a fact snow falls in the mountains.
    I've stood there while it fell
        On me and the temporarily bare stones.
I could see it falling into the broken baffles
    Of granite, hovering on the edge
        Of thawing or staying frozen, both joining
And withholding itself from its other self
    At the confused beginning of spillways
        And misdirected channels and transparently
Aimless pools while it gathered
    And went less often in the wrong directions,
        And I've followed the water down (like it, with no need
To remember where I was or what I was)
    And stood beside its mouth on the ocean shore
        And looked back at the source,
At that stark whiteness. If it all disappears
    Behind clouds this winter, I can be certain
        That where I climbed those steeper and steeper miles
Along its path to the end of trees, to the end
    Of crouching shrubs, to the last of the tendrils
        And wild flowerheads, the same snow is falling.

from *88*

In a Rut

◇ ◇ ◇

She dogs me while
I try to take a catnap.
Of course, I'm playing possum but
I can feel her watching me,
eagle-eyed, like a hawk.
She snakes over to my side
of the bed, and continues to
badger me. I may be a rat, but
I won't let her get my goat.
I refuse to make an
ass of myself, no matter
how mulish I feel.
I'm trying to make a
bee-line for sleep, but
You're a turkey! she says, and
I'm thinking she's no
spring chicken. She *is* a busy beaver,
though, always trying to ferret
things out. She's a bit batty,
in fact, a bit cuckoo, but
What's your beef, now? I say.
*Get your head out
of the sand,* she replies. *What
are you—a man, or a mouse?*
That's a lot of bull, I think;
she can be a real bear.
Don't horse around, now, she says.
You know you can't weasel out of it!
She's having a whale of a time,

thinking she's got me skunked, thinking
that she's out-foxed me.
But I know she's just crying wolf,
and I won't be cowed. Feeling
my oats now, I merely look sheepish;
I give her the hang-dog look;
I give her the lion's share.
I give her something to crow about.
Oh, lovey-dove, I intone.
We're all odd ducks, strange
birds; this won't be my swan-
song, after all. She's in hog-
heaven now, ready to pig-out.
Oh, my stallion, she says, *Oh,
my lambkin! You are
a real animal, you know!*

from *Poetry Northwest*

Premonition

◇   ◇   ◇

It was not yet time
to grow up, & in the growing
vanquish whatever state
of mind to which one
was beholden, the mind freeze
at the end of the alley
where one was stuck
in the wet mud,
where one would remain
forever in the age one was
or stumble onwards
into another time,
a time of being older,
living by the numbers
that kept enlarging, there
was only one number &
as one grew older it grew
larger, the number of
people who were older
than you grew less & it was
not yet time to be who
your mother was, or
(like a dead soldier), the
imprint of your father
in the mud.

★

The hawks & the buzzards
are circling, are singing
our song & all of the heavens
are opening up in quietude

like a prisoner waking
up in solitary confinement
& eating, swallow by swallow,
the crust of bread
under his door,

the hawks & the buzzards making
shadows on the desert
floor, & the leaf of a desert
flower making a shadow
on the sand,

where once I sought out solitude
on the opposite shore,
& rowed beneath the
buzzards' cry with my shoulders
bare,

like a prisoner waking up
before dawn on his bed
of straw, wanting only a glass of water
with the light coming in.

*

Thought moves faster
than my hand can write
like bubbles of water
against the side of a pan.

The flame is light blue,
& the cloud is darkening
at the center, like the pattern
of a dress draped

on a mannequin in someone's
shop. Every time the door
opens a bell rings
& the woman comes out

of the room in the back
to greet her customers
with a smile. Afterwards,
she ridicules them to her

young assistants.

＊

To take responsibility for your life is a middleclass concept. It's
like wearing a neck brace to hide your scars. It means that you're
taking a vow to walk the straight & narrow. The words mean
more than you say, a meal ticket to instant happiness. To articulate
the idea of responsibility indicates an irregular heartbeat. The
label is pinned to your shirt collar, but your true identity has been
erased.

＊

First I had a premonition
that what was happening now would last
a long time, that time could be
measured by motes of dust
which sparkled like colors
in a prism, bursting into flame.

Then, of all my torturers, only myself
remained. Wedged in at first then
unharnessed by doubt or pain.
The insistence flares up again
as in a ravaged heart, I call your name
repeatedly, & into the cold night

the shadows came, staggering
under the weight

of what went before. Only now
could we re-invent a way of telling
the same story, like a stain
that will never wash out,
with no questions asked.

*

There's a pattern in the quilt where you
can run your fingers as if you were looping a
thread or a manacle around your wrist.

The ship lost at sea signals for help.
No one can say whether it was sabotaged
by spies,

or whether its downfall was its own undoing.

*

On the edge of what one might have
once thought of as a possibility
now there's only a narrowing
yet one remains invincible
however tainted by the rush of vehicles
going faster than you
whoever they are are less content

it's the idea of contentment that finally looms large
& settles into its own container
with sediment & growth
until the odor seems strange
& you inflict some damage on the people around you
recovery is swift, retaliation by the numbers
you might think to hole up in a hotel on Broadway

named after an Italian poet whom you can read in the original
but instead you join the spectacular throng
of bespectacled mariners
who cling to the barnacles

on the sides of the rocks
before going under
as the life flow ebbs

★

I wanted to roll up the canopy & go home,
but the customers kept coming. Every time
I decided it was time to close up shop
someone new walked in the door. I wanted to say "We're
closed" but didn't have the heart. Even when I locked
the door someone desperate-looking appeared
at the window, waving her arms excitedly, couldn't wait till
tomorrow. "It's like Xmas here every day," my partner
Olga said, brewing tea on the makeshift hotplate we keep
for nights like tonight, when home is like a mirage which
disappears the closer you get, & dinner waiting on a stove
a memory from someone else's childhood. "Don't ask for anything
—you might get it." The person who said that knew something
I didn't. The smile I use to greet my customers is now my real face.
My parched lips are my parched lips.

★

It was all I could do to drink as much
as possible at one time. So that some kind
of juice might be available in both
cans & bottles & that a new shipment
might arrive by the next train, or else. It
was not what you would call an enviable
position, but thankfully there were others
like me who could understand the dilemma,
no different from looking a gull in the eye,
or glancing the wrong way when crossing the street.
Maybe an overture would be appropriate
to announce victory & a loop of the same songs
on a different radio, the one in my head.
It's always midnight there, & the train
not on time. Orchestral versions of acoustic
dreams quelled anxiety in the emergency

wing. We go on record without fear
of lying to save our friends. We harbor
some handful of truth & disperse.

★

I miss Manhattan, sometimes,
in the morning. But I must admit
I like living on the edge
of the river. When I drive
across the bridge I can see
The World Trade Towers
in the distance. I never thought
I'd want to live anywhere
except the Lower East Side.
Now I can name the people
I know who live there on
the fingers of one hand. It
was where my parents were
born so I always thought
of it as home. A nice place
to visit, but would you want
to live there? The past is all tyranny
& drunkenness, & no one will ever
sleep. All the Gods are out tonight,
patrolling First Avenue in the rain.
"Should I call first or can I just
come over?"

★

Chances are, if you steal
something you're going to be
caught. You might even have
to spend a year or two in
prison. There's always the chance
you might be convicted on

trumped-up charges & receive
a suspended sentence,

but this rarely happens.
Most often, the jury returns
after deliberating for five
minutes.

★

For awhile I wrote poems that entered the labyrinth
& didn't rhyme. The face without lips
I painted was my disguise.

I draw some lightning flashes with my pastels
& the different shades of tonic for where the water
meets the sky.

That was the way I looked then, in colors
that didn't wash out. The way the waves waver on
the edge of the beach & then collapse over my head.

The ring on one finger I painted on as a kind of marriage.
The other ring that disappeared was grafted
to my skin.

Bubbles explode. Heat up the water & turn down
the lights, chain the perambulator to the
garden gate.

I am that shadow at the garden gate, languorous
in my pursuit of lost love, a stranger's heart.
Rumor has it she married for hate.

Dignitaries? Their hair is the same color,
but their skin is mottled. Color their
skin reptilian, & plant the charges.

★

You can say you knew me when,
but I haven't changed. Maybe we spent
a night together & I gave you

my blanket when you were cold.
It was just a thin sheet really, all
that there was.

from *The World*

SUSAN WHEELER

In Sky

◇ ◇ ◇

The high that proved too high, the heroic for earth too hard,
The passion that left the ground to lose itself in the sky . . .
—Robert Browning

The girl is waiting in the room to be discovered.
The girl is attempting radiance.
The girl may be a boy, or vice versa.
The girl is anticipating the man's arrival, later.
The girl is anticipating the man's displeasure.
The girl is anticipating the man's disapproval.
The girl takes no guff.
The girl's mendacity has long been remarked upon.
The girl armors up with *chic.*
The girl carries the blooms, the veronicas, the perovskia.
The girl who may be a boy powders the smalt.

The girl fills the room like smoke.
The girl is a deer in the onrush of lamps, she sits on the planks of the pier.
The girl swings her feet above the surface of the water.

The girl presses out, inhales, still fills her seat not.
The seat is an ink room, not-girl, apprehension.
The girl is mottled with self, with indecision.
The girl's amethyst earrings window her eyes.
The girl twirls her cape before the bull.
She refuses her chest.
She refuses "alabaster."
She refuses your volupty at her expense.

The girl is the hole, the cutout.
The box she is punched from throngs with blue spirits.
The ground is blank as a plum, tank-deep.
O water, o silting of dust. Reticulate.
The room's tonnage sags.
The ground is figure to its own ground.
And she, blade of grass at the Battle at Troy.

The girl refuses the stadium seating.
The girl mixes lazule and vivianite.
The girl was or was not a mother, this is irrelevant.
The girl's skin shelters; her skin burns with self.
At the end of the pier, in the house light, she looks up.
Her shade engulfs her.
The girl's blueism offputs the man.

The Girl look't Blew. Blue funked. Cat indigo.
She yelled bloody blue, she talked a blue streak.
The girl blued her bluebacks on linnets and blue duns.
The girl was waiting to be overtaken.
The girl was cruising for a bruiser.
The girl tilted up at the ciel: blue-domer.
She struck into space like a bolt from the blue.
Azul ultramarino, when I confessed I repented, the girl said.
She was blue mouldy for the want of that drink.

The girl ardent was; ardent, wracked, and replete.
The girl took the *retablo* from the wall; in her hand its wings shone.
The girl watched, as she listened, the strung lights waver.
The girl's moment for radiance passed.
O she was stippled, O but her room was.
O that the treatment take hold and transform.

The girl swung a gun.
The girl jutted her chin fore.
The girl limped with her sidling and stalled.
She has a fast one, it's in a wheel rut, the girl and her blue ruin, gin and her car.
The girl has veined shoulders.
She passes wind.

The girl's form is landmined: flounces, the flesh.
The girl bats the red lock away from her ear.
The girl takes the synapse and invests it with *scene* (insensible sense).
The girl Rapunzel is (*NOT*). She disdains.

O discrete make me and blocked.
O scurry me forth on the slate patio, and applaud my every squeak.
O I am helpful like a shill (no groin).
Untransmutable plane with your shadowed door.
The room heats like a vise.

The girl splices the water like a seal or a grouper.
The girl's shell grows a rubbery skin.
The girl looks right back, planted.

The girl holds her thumb piano beneath our view.

She, the girl, regards the chimpanzee.
The chamber loses its ceiling and the stars prick through.

The girl breathes. Her sex bucks out of sight.

The girl, blushing: *O did you see me there? Did you?*

from *Boston Review*

Man Running

◇　◇　◇

Whatever he has done
Against our law and peace of mind,
Our mind's eye looks with pity of a kind
At the scared, stumbling fellow on the run

Who hears a siren scream
As through the thickets we conceive
He plows with fending arms, and to deceive
The snuffling dogs now flounders up a stream

Until he doubles back,
Climbing at length a rocky rise
To where he crumples and, exhausted, lies
In the scorched brush beside a railroad track.

★

If then he hops a freight
And clatteringly rides as far
As the next county in a cattle car,
We feel our sense of him disintegrate

In rumors, warnings, claims
That here or there he has appeared—
Tall, short, fierce, furtive, with or without a beard.
Still, in fidelity to childhood games

And outlaws of romance,
We darkly cheer him, whether or not

He robbed that store, or bank, or fired that shot,
And wish him, guiltily, a sporting chance.

·

Ditching the stolen truck,
He disappears into a vast
Deep-wooded wilderness, and is at last
Beyond the reach of law, and out of luck,

And we are one with him,
Sharing with him that eldest dread
Which, when it gathers in a sleeping head,
Is a place mottled, ominous, and dim

Remembered from the day
When we descended from the trees
Into the shadow of our enemies,
Not lords of nature yet, but naked prey.

from *The New Yorker*

C . K . W I L L I A M S

The World

◊   ◊   ◊

Splendid that I'd revel even more in the butterflies harvesting pollen
from the lavender in my father-in-law's garden in Normandy
when I bring to mind Francis Ponge's poem where he transfigures them
to levitating matches, and the flowers they dip into to unwashed cups;
it doesn't work with lavender, but still, so lovely, matches, cups,
and lovely, too, to be here in the fragrant summer sunlight reading.

Just now an essay in *Le Monde,* on Fragonard, his oval oil sketch
of a mother opening the bodice of her rosily blushing daughter
to demonstrate to a young artist that the girl would be suitable as a "model";
the snide quotation marks insinuate she might be other than she seems,
but to me she seems entirely enchanting, even without her top
and with the painter's cane casually lifting her skirt from her ankle.

Fragonard needs so little for his plot; the girl's disarranged underslips
a few quick swirls, the mother's compliant mouth a blur, her eyes
two dots of black, yet you can see how crucial this transaction is to her,
how accommodating she'd be in working through potential complications.
In the shadows behind, a smear of fabric spills from a drawer,
a symbol surely, though when one starts thinking symbol, what isn't?

Each sprig of lavender lifting jauntily as its sated butterfly departs,
Catherine beneath the beech tree with her father and sisters, me watching,
everything and everyone might stand for something else, *be* something else.
Though in truth I can't imagine what; reality has put itself so solidly before me
there's little need for mystery. . . . Except for us, for how we take the world
to us, and make it more, more than we are, more even than itself.

from *The New Yorker*

My Work

◇ ◇ ◇

In my work, at any given point,
the great issues of identity politics
and dialectical absolutism assume
a tight coherence, a profoundly
threatening total awareness
by which I seek to mediate
the conflict between meaning
and the extremes of deconstruction.

I never strike a false note.
I believe in savvy artistic
incandescence as a constitutive
enhancement of racy sexuality,
all as a way to examine the
necessity of self-love.

It's always dangerous to underestimate
my work. I insult the intellectual
dignity of the French. They arrive
in my brightly colored landscape
right after quitting time only to discover
an empty stage set in which all the clueless
actors have wandered off to an installation
of obsolete Marxist sloganeering.

Yeats was deeply immersed in mythology
and so am I. T. S. Eliot preferred Dante
to Shakespeare, but I don't. Charles Bernstein
loves the way my sentences decompose.

John Ashbery will read my work only
while naked. Everything I do is the pure
output of brains, speed, and skill.

A couple of weeks ago, I digested
Aristotle. I found him to be electrifyingly
ahistorical, and he now has been subsumed
into my work. I have open-ended stratagems
when it comes to the Germans, particularly
Goethe and Kant. They live now in my
imagination. I go way beyond alienation
into a new synthesis of desire and content.

My work stands for something invisible,
something inner. I attempt to explain
the risk of appearing. Foucault would know
how well my work succeeds in revealing
the discourse between power and structure.
When you read my work, you may think
"simile" or "metaphor," but what you really
get is the storm, the dark mansion, the servant
girl standing alone in Columbus Circle.

Triumph and loss permeate my work.
People should try to pick up on that.
My technical virtuosity is unrivaled.
Don't talk to me about subject matter.
My work takes "narrative" and turns
it into what never happened. In my work,
"story" becomes language contemplating
its own articulation in a field of gesture.

There is a higher reality at play in my work.
Sacred memories resonate with perceptual
knowledge of the body as primal text. Yet
my work is never subservient to the dominant
ideology. It circulates warmly and freely
through all available channels. My work
is like the furniture you so much want to
sink into, but must wait as it wends its way

from distant points in a giant moving truck
screeching across the country
to your new home.

from *New American Writing*

Scrabble with Matthews

◇ ◇ ◇

Jerboa on a triple: I was in for it,
my *zither* on a double looking feeble

as a "promising" first book. Oedipal & reckless,
my scheme would fail: keep him a couple drinks

ahead, & perhaps the muse would smile
upon me with some *ses* or some blanks.

January, Vermont: snowflakes teased the windows
of the Burlington airport bar. The waitress

tallied tips & channel-surfed above the amber
stutter of the snowplow's light: it couldn't

keep up, either. Visibility to zero, nothing taking off
& his *dulcimer* before me (50 bonus points

for "bingos") like a cautionary tale. The night
before I'd been his warm up act,

the audience of expensive preppies
doubling to twenty when he shambled

to the podium to give them Martial
& his then-new poems. "Why do you write

something nobody reads anymore?" queried one
little trust fund in a blazer. "Because

I'm willing to be honestly confused
& honestly fearful." *Il miglior fabbro,*

a.k.a. *Prez:* sweet & fitting honorifics he has left
upon the living's lips. Sweet & fitting too

that I could know the poems much better than
the man, flawed as I am told he was. Connoisseur

of word-root & amphibrach, of Coltrane
solo & of California reds, of box score & Horatian loss,

his garrulousness formidable & masking
a shyness I could never penetrate, meeting him

would always find me tongue-tied,
minding my *ps* & *qs*, the latter of which

I could not play, failing three times to draw a *u.*
The dead care nothing for our eulogies:

he wrote this many times & well.
& yet I pray his rumpled *daimonion*

shall guide our letters forward
as they wend the snow-white notebook leaves,

the stanzas scrolling down the laptop screens.
Game after game & the snow labored on.

Phalanx, bourboned whiteout & the board aglow
as he'd best me again & again. *Qintar*

& *prosody,* the runway lights enshrouded
& the wind, *endquote,* shook the panes.

from *Poetry*

Clemency

◇　◇　◇

Over the trough, the long face of the horse,
and croaking dead center in a hoofprint,
a toad—all the while the redwing blackbirds
drilling their whistly bells. February,
and a sudden, unearthly spring. God above me,
I am halfway through this field, a feeding,
the season, my life. If it pleases you, then hear me:
what I would ask is ten thousand more afternoons
like this, though doubtless the unkilled fleas, scintillate
and fat, will bedevil the dogs and cats,
and a few, blood-weary, will fall among
the rumpled bedclothes to catch us there,
my lover and me, and marry us done.
But please, just let this long light be garlanded by bird
and the garrulous, sloe-eyed toad.
Let the mare scratch her ear all down the length of me.
Let her breathe where the lick of memory wants.

from *The Kenyon Review*

After the Opening, 1932

◇ ◇ ◇

Why hadn't he thought of it before?
He turns to Jo, to the waiter handing out
buttered rolls, glasses of wine, caviar:
everyone must go! He realizes chairs
should remain in disarray, windows open,
gleaming ends of rump roast steaks and salmon
pâtés cooling in neglected browns and pinks.

At the Whitney, earlier, he was approached
by a small man with a quivering grin.
If you don't mind my saying so, he began,
but Hopper did, and turned to admire
his lost faces, lights flirting with darks,
the tip of a steeple just brushing the sky.
You've really got it, you know—
what it's like when no one's around.
Hopper took an inward bow, then noticed
the white tied bow in *New York Restaurant,*
quiet blue back and perched beige vase towering
over a *Room in Brooklyn,* where light
and afternoon would have done.

It will not do! He can scarcely eat;
Jo chats with the Rockefellers,
the Pierpont Morgans, Guggenheims,
while Hopper's lost in an empty room.
From now on, he vows, all will be absence—

shadows the dreams of long gone men,
roads into the distance only roads, eyes
only eyes, with nothing behind them.

from *The Threepenny Review*

Reading the Bones:
a Blackjack Moses nightmare

◇   ◇   ◇

He squatted down
on the sidewalk
in front of my home

"this ground is a footprint
of your life," He said

As he took his bones from a bag
made of snake skin

He tossed them on my paved ground,
spread them out like a map,
studied them like a book:

What he saw in those old bones
made him scream, the sound
voiced from somewhere
deep within, forcing me to quick-step back
as he leaped to his feet
ran like terror after madness
down the sidewalk of my tribe

I stared the distance after him,
then looked down at his forgotten bones,
wondering if I should pick them up,
not wanting to touch them

tho they already touched something frightening,
something standing like a skeleton
of my own bones
dressed in nightmare
waiting to be read.

from *American Poetry Review*

CONTRIBUTORS' NOTES AND COMMENTS

JONATHAN AARON was born in Northampton, Massachusetts, in 1941. His two books of poems are *Second Sight* (Harper & Row, 1982) and *Corridor* (Wesleyan/New England, 1992). He teaches writing and literature at Emerson College.

Aaron writes: " 'The End of *Out of the Past*' contains a compressed version of the final ten minutes of the noir classic (1947) directed by Jacques Tourneur and starring Robert Mitchum, Jane Greer, and Kirk Douglas. *Out of the Past* makes the case that color in film is beside the point. As you watch the movie, prepare yourself for the brief view of Lake Tahoe at dusk that presages what's in store for Jeff Bailey (Mitchum), a good guy who can't escape his past, and the murderous Kathie Moffett (Greer), who thinks she finally has him to herself. Though you see it only for a moment, the scenery is monumental, like something out of Alfred Bierstadt. It has the effect of making you realize the futility of the characters' efforts to make something out of their lives.

"*Out of the Past* is a first-rate work of art—every time I see it I recognize things in it I hadn't seen before. Or things I'd seen before but now see in a new way. On one occasion when I watched the movie, it occurred to me that I was a little boy when the movie was being made, and that while these actors were playing the characters who were living out the movie's plot (and in particular its final moments) we were all actually sharing a specific moment in time, no matter that they were in California and I was this five-year-old on the east coast who thought there were monsters under his bed. What a world, I thought. Then the last line came to me."

BETH ANDERSON was born in Daly City, California, in 1968. Since receiving an MFA from Brown University, she has worked as an editor and lexicographer in Boston and Richmond, Virginia, where she currently lives. She is the author of *The Habitable World,* published in 2001 by Instance Press, and a collection entitled *Overboard,* forthcoming from Burning Deck.

Anderson writes: "The locked room contains an impossible crime. John Dickson Carr, a master of the locked-room mystery, sets murders in the center of muddy tennis courts devoid of all but the victim's footprints and in rooms with barred windows and doors sealed from the inside with deadbolt locks. 'A Locked Room' was written out of my interest in how these crimes are rendered 'impossible,' despite their completion, by the structure of their stories. I wanted to work with the idea that poems and mysteries both benefit from devices like red herrings, which might frustrate readers who are focused on finding a solution but are indispensable to those of us taken with the process of investigation."

NIN ANDREWS was born in Charlottesville, Virginia, in 1958. She is the author of *Spontaneous Breasts* (Pearl Press, 1997), *Why They Grow Wings* (Silverfish Press, 2000), *The Book of Orgasms* (Cleveland State University Press, 2000), and *Any Kind of Excuse* (Kent State University Press, 2003). *The Book of Orgasms and Other Tales,* a new and enlarged edition of her first book, appeared in 2003 from Bloodaxe Books in England. She lives in Poland, Ohio.

Of "Dedicated to the One I Love," Andrews writes: "When I wrote this poem, I was feeling hopeless and uninspired and flipping through books, reading about the New York poets like Frank O'Hara, who could write a poem on a whim. I also remember reading that the muse is always female. Not mine. I've always imagined the muse as some kind of asshole lover (a clone of James Dean) I try to win back again and again. I began to wonder why people assign gender to certain divinities such as muses and angels. And to contemplate the desire for desire itself, the wish to catch fire, what the Hasidim call *hitlahavut,* without which not even heaven is paradise, but with which the most ordinary event is transcendent. . . .

"There were other thoughts going through my head. Aren't there always too many thoughts? I was contemplating Buddhist teachings about living in the present, the Buddhist version of *carpe diem.* I began to wonder if it might be possible to live backwards, to reverse time, or even to be fully present in the past. Who, after all, lives in the present? Who, unlike Orpheus, can resist the urge to look back? To wonder what could have been, and if convenient, to revise the scenery, create alternate histories? Even if I resist the temptation, the mind is but a door. Anyone can come in, and the most seductive are frequent guests. Like James

Dean. Thinking is an ongoing process, and the light in the mind never shuts off. Someone is often lounging around in there, making love or eating bonbons or telling secrets. It's so sad when I remind myself that Dean is dead, and I'm alone in an empty room with nothing but a leaky roof and words I can't quite recall. Something I mean to say but never can."

WENDELL BERRY was born in Henry County, Kentucky, in 1934. He is a writer and farmer, whose most recent books are *Selected Poems* (1998), *A Timbered Choir* (poems, 1998), *Jayber Crow* (a novel, 2000), and *The Art of the Commonplace* (essays, 2002), all from Counterpoint Press.

FRANK BIDART was born in Bakersfield, California, in 1939. He recently edited, with David Gewanter, *The Collected Poems of Robert Lowell,* for Farrar, Straus and Giroux. In 2002 he published a chapbook, *Music Like Dirt,* with Sarabande. His earlier books, including *Desire* (1997) and *In the Western Night: Collected Poems 1965–1990* (1991) are available from Farrar, Straus and Giroux.

Of "Curse," Bidart writes: "The 'you' addressed here brought down the World Trade Center towers; when I wrote the poem I didn't imagine that it could be read any other way, though it has been. The poem springs from the ancient moral idea (the idea of Dante's *Divine Comedy*) that what is suffered for an act should correspond to the nature of the act. Shelley in his 'Defense of Poetry' says that 'the great secret of morals is love'—and by love he means not affection or erotic feeling, but sympathetic identification, identification with others. The 'secret,' hidden ground of how to act morally is entering the skin of another, imagination of what is experienced as the result of the act. Identification is here called down as punishment, the great secret of morals reduced to a curse."

DIANN BLAKELY was born in Anniston, Alabama, in 1957. Her first collection, *Hurricane Walk,* appeared in 1992 from BOA editions and was listed as one of the year's ten best books by the *St. Louis Post-Dispatch. Farewell, My Lovelies,* her second book, was released by Story Line Press in 2000. A third manuscript, *Cities of Flesh and the Dead,* won the Alice Fay di Castagnola Award from the Poetry Society of America. Her new project is a cycle of "duets," or call-and-response poems, with the thirty-three known songs of the great bluesman Robert Johnson. She is a poetry editor of *Antioch Review* and an arts reviewer for the *Nashville Scene*/Village Voice Media Group.

Of "Rambling on My Mind," Blakely writes: "Robert Johnson is a presence for anyone interested in American vernacular music, but his absences and disappearances are equally crucial to the genius of his art and its legacy. Recent official attempts to define Johnson have been particularly ludicrous, from the airbrushing of the dangling cigarette in the infamous stamp portrait to the establishment of his estate's inheritor via testimony from his alleged aunt, who, after a fish fry, was busy with one Saturday-night gentleman friend in a ditch while her sister was conceiving Johnson in a similar ditch just a few feet away.

"The sublime has risen from greater depths, as I think even Virgil would agree in regard to Johnson's conception, and also in regard to that spookily monumental photograph, thought to be the second of the only two pictures we have of him, taken in a dime store not long before his death. Like the Roman poet, Johnson sang with authority, in part, because his voice is fully human and—paradoxically—because he seems to sound the notes that most of us hear only on the other side.

"When I began writing these poems, I knew that my family had owned slaves in the eighteenth and nineteenth centuries, a knowledge that quickly came to seem insufficient. Yet I thought that any particulars I found would be pretty generic, if nonetheless shameful. I did not expect to learn that one of my forebears was the first woman killed in the Nat Turner insurrection of 1831; that another, a wealthy Virginia landowner and anti-slavery activist, attempted to establish a manumission plantation in Alabama in hopes of demonstrating a personal and practical means of ending what he called 'the sorest and most afflictive evil of our day & generation'; or that his son and nephew, both Civil War combatants, committed suicide, the former on Christmas Day of 1861.

"The dead, when approached closely enough, will always spurn the definitions with which we try to capture them, even if, to us, a definition feels like an embrace rather than a violation. Even if, to us, the present tense seems to enfold every moment of the past that we can imagine; and, simultaneously, the songs of all souls originate in a realm beyond anything like time."

BRUCE BOND was born in Pasadena, California, in 1954. After receiving his master's degree in music performance from Lamont School of Music and working for years as a classical and jazz guitarist, he went on to earn a Ph.D. in English from the University of Denver in 1987. His collections of poetry include *Cinder* (Etruscan Press, 2003), *The Throats of Narcissus* (University of Arkansas, 2001), *adiography* (Ornish Award, BOA Editions, 1997), *The Anteroom of Paradise* (Colladay Award, QRL,

1991), and *Independence Days* (R. Gross Award, Woodley Press, 1990). He is a professor of English at the University of North Texas and poetry editor of *American Literary Review*.

Bond writes: "As part of the sequence entitled 'Solo Sessions,' the poem 'Art Tatum' is one among several that explores themes of hardship, alienation, and imaginative transfiguration in the lives and music of various jazz musicians. In each case I chose an artist whose music I loved: someone whose dire circumstance and isolation inspired a consequent intimacy with the elements of creative discipline and play. Each suffered some form of deprivation or trauma that made for an abiding wound or limitation, but likewise a reservoir of expressive and compensatory energies, of possible strides, rebellions, affirmations. As with all resourceful artists, they entrusted themselves to a tradition, yes, but one that places a high value on spontaneous and dissonant willfulness—a kind of signing the air with something distinct, ephemeral, self-constructing, self-negating, generous, compelled.

"The story of Art Tatum, fluent wizard, the dazzling champion at so many 'cutting sessions' of his time, is a tale of remarkable sympathies, beginning with the odd contagion of blindness as it traveled from his wounded eye to its untouched twin. The world of sound became even more deeply internalized for him, even more vital, especially as it lit out from his own fingertips, his music sweet and lithe, animating, Orphean in its power to raise up, as if by faith, to illuminate, to praise."

CATHERINE BOWMAN was born in El Paso, Texas, in 1957. She lives in Bloomington, Indiana, where she teaches in the MFA program at Indiana University. She is the author of two collections of poems, *1-800-HOT-RIBS* (Gibbs Smith, 1993) and *Rock Farm* (Gibbs Smith, 1996). She is also the editor of *Word of Mouth: Poems Featured on NPR's* All Things Considered (Vintage, 2003).

Of "1000 Lines," Bowman writes: "*Numerology: the study of the occult meaning of numbers and their supposed influence on human life.* I started out this poem imagining a pseudo-numerologist, an initiate into a secret society of language where secrets bubble up underneath words from a realm that can only be accessed and revealed through the powers of 10. The poem ended up being instead an homage to a marriage, ten years, music, and New York City and an exercise in forgetting and remembering. In hindsight, the structure, the gridlike stanzas, even the word ten seemed to become for me containers, cribs, crypts, and mini-storage units filled with fragments and things that served my obsessive attempts to retrieve the irretrievable past and my concurrent and convenient escapes from the same enterprise. The poem became an exploration into why things happen the way they do, and the answer I discovered through my forays into formulaic computations is that there is no answer—concealed and locked away as it is forever in the numeral ten. I wrote much of the poem on index cards and sometimes like to randomly shuffle the order around. Thirty-three of the poem's 100 stanzas are included here."

ROSEMARY CATACALOS was born in St. Petersburg, Florida, in 1944, and raised in San Antonio, Texas, where her family has had deep roots since the early 1900s. Of Mexican and Greek descent, she is the author of a chapbook, *As Long As It Takes* (Iguana Press, St. Louis, 1984) and a full-length collection, *Again for the First Time* (Tooth of Time Books, Santa Fe, 1984). She has been a writing fellow of the National Endowment for the Arts, the Texas Institute of Letters/University of Texas at Austin, and the Stegner program at Stanford University. A former executive director of the Poetry Center and American Poetry Archives at San Francisco State University, she is currently an affiliated scholar at Stanford University's Institute for Research on Women and Gender, where she is working on a new collection of poems and gathering transition stories from Mexican immigrant women.

Of "Perfect Attendance: Short Subjects Made from the Staring Photos of Strangers," Catacalos writes: "A brooch by Chicago art jeweler Kiff Slemmons informed this poem. Also called 'Perfect Attendance,' Slemmons's piece features seven pairs of eyes, excised from dusky vintage portraits, protected with a layer of mica, and hinged one above the other in silver frames so that the shape of the completed piece recalls a school attendance medal.

"A meticulous artist whose work reflects a challenging narrative complexity and love of language, Slemmons has also created a series of brooches representing hands, which echo in the poem. Even the silver-rimmed keys of my tenth stanza are found in her work, though in her case they belong to a typewriter.

"Slemmons is adroit at wordplay. I read her 'Perfect Attendance' brooch as a celebration of the specific subjects and the way they now seem to be paying close attention to the viewer. The implied question is: are *we* attending to the world as closely as we can?

"My poem wants to speak to the strong sense of rescue I feel in Slemmons's work. I hope that my suggestions set off a similarly intricate chain of associations in the reader, so that the process of rescue through remembrance (and close attention) is passed along, as it has been from Slemmons to me.

"One of the reasons Slemmons's work engages me so deeply is that my family, on my maternal grandfather Peñaloza's side, has produced four generations of jewelers.

"Finally, it turns out Slemmons and I both are drawn to the work of Eadweard Muybridge (1830–1904), the British artist, photographer, and inventor, whose elaborate photographic motion studies, many of horses, are widely acknowledged as having pioneered the motion picture industry."

JOSHUA CLOVER was born in Berkeley, California, in 1962.

Of "Aeon Flux: June," Clover writes: "In composing this poem, I was thinking on a line-by-line basis of Jeff Clark's poem 'Jade Ache.' "

BILLY COLLINS was born in New York City in 1941. His books of poetry include *Nine Horses* (Random House, 2002), *Sailing Alone Around the Room: New and Selected Poems* (Random House, 2001), *Picnic, Lightning* (University of Pittsburgh Press, 1998), *The Art of Drowning* (University of Pittsburgh Press, 1995), and *Questions About Angels* (William Morrow, 1991), which was selected for the National Poetry Series by Edward Hirsch and reprinted by the University of Pittsburgh Press in 1999. He has won the Bess Hokin Prize, the Frederick Bock Prize, the Oscar Blumenthal Prize, and the Levinson Prize—all awarded by *Poetry* magazine. A recipient of a Guggenheim Fellowship and a grant from the National Endowment for the Arts, he is a Distinguished Professor of English at Lehman College (City University of New York). This is his eighth appearance in *The Best American Poetry*. He is serving a two-year term as United States Poet Laureate.

Collins writes: "Although more than twice the length of a sonnet, 'Litany' is a burlesque of certain sonnet conventions, mainly the Petrarchan habit of flattering the beloved by comparing her to various delights found in nature. Such blandishments are deflated here as the speaker quickly turns to consider what the beloved is *not*. The poem also exemplifies the sonneteer's tendency to swing attention away from the beloved and toward himself, a narcissistic reflex that often occurs at the so-called turn. You may be the bread and the knife, but I am the sound of rain on the roof. So there.

"As for Jacques Crickillon, I had not heard of him before coming across his poem in a magazine. The contributors' page simply noted that

'Jacques Crickillon lives in Belgium.' Last year in Mexico, I happened to meet the great poet Hugo Claus, who still lives in his native Belgium. When I inquired after M. Crickillon, Claus said that, yes, he was not only a poet but a professional bicycle racer and then went on to expound on the compatibility of the two pursuits."

MICHAEL S. COLLINS was born in Kingston, Jamaica, in 1959. He has spent most of his life in the United States but has also worked in China and Singapore. In addition to poems, he has published essays and scholarly articles on such subjects as the United Nations, altruism, Alan Greenspan, contemporary poetry, and the relationships between literature and economics. He is currently assistant professor of English at Texas A&M University in College Station.

Of "Six Sketches: When a Soul Breaks," Collins writes: "My favorite works of art offer pictures of human choice. Michelangelo's *Last Judgment,* Yeats's 'Long-Legged Fly,' Jimi Hendrix's 'Star-Spangled Banner,' and productions of various living masters—such mind-openers are too exalted to be emulated. Yet they haunt my days and my pen. They hover over and probably obliterate a poem like 'Sketches.'

"For what it's worth, however, the ruminations and writings out of which 'Sketches' grew have to do with the ways in which credit—from Latin *credere,* to believe—beats at the heart of language, economics, and deception.

"The poem is full of emblems of such things. In the back of the mind as I wrote were, section by section, 1) double agents Robert Hanssen and Aldrich Aimes; 2) a prostitute described by Louis Armstrong in *Satchmo: My Life in New Orleans;* 3) Sylvia Plath; 4) Jimi Hendrix (crucial, because the sestina form around which 'Sketches' is built is a feedback device par excellence, and Hendrix was the great magician of feedback).

"Section five of the poem extrapolates from Friedrich Nietzsche, who wrote, in Walter Kaufman's translation, that 'Buying and selling, together with their psychological appurtenances, are older even than the beginning of any kind of social forms of organizations and alliances.' Section six of 'Sketches' flits from the Dutch tulip mania to a Nick Leeson–like bank killer to executives fit for Enron, to a Robert Mugabe–like dictator."

CARL DENNIS was born in St. Louis, Missouri, in 1939. He lives in Buffalo, where he is artist-in-residence at the State University of New York, and has served on the faculty of the graduate writing program at

Warren Wilson College. In 2000 he was awarded the Ruth Lilly Prize for his contribution to American poetry. His most recent book of poetry, *Practical Gods* (Penguin, 2001), won the 2002 Pulitzer Prize in poetry.

Dennis writes: "In 'World History' I try to use an unfashionable tradition to provide enough distance on fashionable political discourse to suggest how much it omits from its calculations."

SUSAN DICKMAN was born in Chicago, Illinois, in 1963. She majored in English at the University of Illinois, Urbana-Champaign, and received an MFA in writing at the University of California. She is currently teaching middle school. In 1998 she received an Illinois Arts Council Award in fiction. A mother of three, she has completed a novel, two poetry manuscripts, and a collection of short stories. Much of her subject matter derives from her "years of travel, physical and psychic, spiritual and political, within and among Israel's multilayered, intersecting diasporas of cultural longing, language, history, and myth."

Dickman writes: " 'Skin' came to me in one draft in the form of a meditation or prayer, as a way to contain the horror and drama of what is now rather casually known as a suicide bombing. What struck me each time I watched the television coverage of a bombing were the religious men in the background working quickly and diligently, searching for bits of skin in accordance with the biblical edict that no human flesh be left unburied. It is strange to consider that minutes after a bomb explodes, a corps of men arrives to begin the work of picking up every shred of human biological evidence; once the bomb has gone off, flesh is merely flesh and cares nothing for nationality, ethnic identity, or argument over homeland. I often wonder what the men are thinking—are they thinking? are they praying?—as they gather for burial the mixed flesh of bombers and victims, all children of God. The repetition of ritual and the focus on the physical—the skin itself—was my way of mediating the reality that horror, particularly when viewed through the lens of the media, rapidly becomes banal. I wrote the poem simply in order to remember that on some level, if present only as a television viewer and a lover of one blessed and cursed region on this earth, I was a witness."

RITA DOVE was born in Akron, Ohio, in 1952. Her poetry collections include *The Yellow House on the Corner* (Carnegie Mellon University Press, 1980), *Museum* (Carnegie Mellon, 1983), *Thomas and Beulah* (Carnegie Mellon, 1986), *Grace Notes* (W. W. Norton, 1989), *Selected Poems* (Pantheon/Vintage, 1993), *Mother Love* (Norton, 1995), and *On the Bus with*

Rosa Parks (Norton, 1999). She has also written a book of short stories, *Fifth Sunday* (Callaloo Fiction Series, 1985); a novel, *Through the Ivory Gate* (Pantheon, 1992); a volume of essays, *The Poet's World* (The Library of Congress, 1995); and a play, *The Darker Face of the Earth* (Story Line Press, 2000), which had its world premiere in 1996 at the Oregon Shakespeare Festival and was subsequently produced at the Kennedy Center in Washington, D.C., and the Royal National Theatre in London. In 1987 she received the Pulitzer Prize in poetry, and from 1993 to 1995 she served as poet laureate of the United States. She has received twenty honorary doctorates. Her new collection of poetry, *American Smooth,* is due out in 2004. She is Commonwealth Professor of English at the University of Virginia in Charlottesville, where she lives with her husband, the German-born writer Fred Viebahn. She was the guest editor of *The Best American Poetry 2000.*

Of "Fox Trot Fridays," Dove writes: "A few weeks after our house was struck by lightning and burned down, my husband and I found ourselves at a formal dinner dance which concerned neighbors had arranged for us to attend. We'd spent every waking moment sifting through the debris, salvaging charred manuscripts, and the like; the only clothes we owned were donated or bought quickly at WalMart—sneakers, khakis, T-shirts. 'Enough already!' our neighbors declared. 'This weekend you're coming with us; go buy yourselves something pretty!' So we did. And there we sat, resplendent in tux and blue sequins, enjoying ourselves, when this amazing couple floated by, dancing the most ethereal waltz I'd ever seen. Even before the dessert dishes (strawberry cheesecake) could be cleared away, we and our wonderful neighbors had decided to sign up for a free introductory lesson at the local dance studio. Fred and I were the only couple to keep it up—dancing on the ashes, as it were—perhaps, at first, because learning something entirely frivolous and beautiful was a welcome distraction from the sorrow we were working through at the time. A year later, our house finally stood again, new and improved, on its old foundations. But we've kept on dancing."

STEPHEN DUNN was born in Forest Hills, New York, in 1939. He teaches creative writing at Richard Stockton College of New Jersey. His twelve books of poetry include *Local Visitations* (W. W. Norton, 2003) and *Different Hours* (Norton), which won the 2001 Pulitzer Prize. A new and expanded edition of *Walking Light: Essays & Memoirs* was recently published by BOA Editions.

Dunn writes: "I hesitate to indicate the specific emotional underpinnings of 'Open Door Blues.' They're more trivial, I suspect, than what the poem itself suggests. Moreover, they might belie what were my primary compositional concerns: to find language and rhythms equivalent to a mood. In other words, no matter what I was feeling I had some linguistic fun being bluesy."

STUART DYBEK was born in Chicago, Illinois, in 1942. He studied poetry and fiction at the Iowa Writers' Workshop, and currently teaches in the writing program at Western Michigan University and in the Prague Summer Workshops. His books of poetry include *Brass Knuckles* (Carnegie Mellon University Press, 2003) and the forthcoming *Streets in Their Own Ink* (Farrar, Straus and Giroux, 2004).

Of "Journal," Dybek writes: "A moment arrives—seemingly of its own accord—when one becomes aware of constructing a book, rather than simply accumulating individual pieces for a collection. Motifs are suddenly obvious, and repeated images, and suggestions of a narrative—fragmented or ghostly though it may be. There are voices in monologue that, given the chance, might engage in dialogues, and themes on which to base variations, and points waiting for counterpoint. Unfinished books have a way of demanding what's necessary to make them complete, of generating new poems that the writer might not have felt compelled to write without the demand of form. 'Journal' was such a poem. It's one of the last I wrote for a book whose working title was *Anti-Memoir*—a title that, unfortunately for me, André Malraux got to first. Though it's no longer my title, it served as a guide for exploring—and for treating as metaphors—related literary forms: autobiography, diaries, letters, notebooks, confessions, journals. One can't help noticing the affinity for the memoir that poets have shown in recent decades. Is there a special relationship between poetry and these 'real life' forms, a relationship closer than, say, between poetry and fiction? Fiction admits to being a lie. What admission, if any, is implicit in a memoir, an autobiography, a journal?"

CHARLES FORT was born in New Britain, Connecticut, in 1951. He holds an endowed chair in poetry at the University of Nebraska at Kearney. His books include *The Town Clock Burning* (1991, reprinted in the Carnegie Mellon University Press Classic Contemporary Series), *Darvil* (St. Andrews Press, 1985), and *Frankenstein Was a Negro (Darvil: Book Two)* (Logan House Press, 2002). *We Did Not Fear the Father, As the Lilac Burned the Laurel Grew, Immortelles, Afro Psalms, Blues of a Mumbling Train,* and *The Poet's Wife* were all published by the University of Nebraska at Kearney Press. He is completing a film documentary on his hometown, once called "The Hardware City of the World." His work appeared in *The Best American Poetry 2000*.

Fort writes: " 'The Vagrant Hours' is not a mere calendar of genres or a reckless treatise on the creative process. I attempted to meld a narrative thread within variant forms, always a wheelbarrow task for any closet formalist. Form assists the intuitive journey on the precarious cliff with a flared tongue toward heaven and hell. Form is a rhetorical vessel, a velvet bag found in the back pocket of the drowned poet, images and jewels on the gangplank after the last great dive, shipwrecked on the landscape of the heart's repair. I end with the concluding lines from one of my variant sonnets: 'Salieri breeds his own cross and crown/Amadeus hears the singing of the earthmen and their ruby dolls.' "

JAMES GALVIN was born in Chicago, Illinois, in 1951, and was raised in northern Colorado. He now has some land, a house, and some horses outside of Tie Siding, Wyoming, and is a member of the permanent faculty at the University of Iowa Writers' Workshop. His books include *Resurrection Update: Collected Poems 1975–1997* (Copper Canyon) and two prose works, *The Meadow* (1992) and *Fencing the Sky* (1999), published by Henry Holt. *X: Poems* was published this year by Copper Canyon.

AMY GERSTLER was born in San Diego, California, in 1956. Her books of poetry include *Medicine* (Penguin Putnam, 2000), *Crown of Weeds* (Viking Penguin, 1997), *Nerve Storm* (Viking Penguin, 1993), and *Bitter Angel* (North Point Press, 1990; Carnegie-Mellon University Press, 1997). *Bitter Angel* won the National Book Critics Circle Award in 1991. She teaches in the Bennington Writing Seminars Program in Bennington, Vermont, and at Art Center College of Design in Pasadena, California. She has a book of poems forthcoming from Penguin in 2004. She lives in Los Angeles.

Of "An Offer Received in this Morning's Mail:," Gerstler writes: "Mishearings and misreadings often provide valuable and unexpected inspiration for poems. I went out to get the mail one groggy morning and did in fact misread copy on an ad for a set of CDs of Beethoven's Complete Symphonies, thinking that the last word in the phrase was 'sympathies,' and marveling for a confused moment that such a useful, elusive commodity was now available for purchase. Poor Beethoven had a grim life in many ways, and did write beautiful, highly emotional letters like the one quoted from in the poem, and these were sources I drew on in writing this piece."

LOUISE GLÜCK was born in New York City in 1943. She has written ten books of poetry, the most recent of which is *The Seven Ages* (Ecco, 2001). Her collection of essays, *Proofs and Theories* (Ecco, 1995), won the PEN–Martha Albrand Award. She has also received the Pulitzer Prize, the Bobbitt National Poetry Prize, the National Book Critics Circle Award, and the Bollingen Prize. She teaches at Williams College and lives in Cambridge, Massachusetts. She was guest editor of *The Best American Poetry 1993*.

MICHAEL GOLDMAN was born in New York in 1936, where he lives with his wife, Eleanor Bergstein. He has published two volumes of poetry, *First Poems* and *At the Edge,* both from Macmillan. Of his books of prose, two have won the George Jean Nathan Award for dramatic criticism, while another was nominated for the National Book Award. His most recent book is *On Drama: Boundaries of Genre, Borders of Self.* He is professor of English emeritus at Princeton University.

Goldman writes: "A large portion of 'Report on Human Beings' was written relatively quickly over several days or hours; the rest took relatively long, several years. I had been writing a number of poems about last judgments and ultimate exams. There came into my head the question of how one might describe human beings to rational creatures who were not human and had no direct contact with us—our successors, presumably. So I had to think about what was distinctively human.

"As far as I can remember, the premise of the poem preceded any of its lines, which is unusual for me. For the form, I went back to a kind of loose, 'breathing' stanza I first used in a poem called 'Elevation 800 Feet,' whose title suggests the kind of middle style I was aiming for."

RAY GONZALEZ was born in El Paso, Texas, in 1952. He is the author of seven books of poetry, including three from BOA Editions: *The Heat of Arrivals* (1997), *Cabato Sentora* (2000), and *The Hawk Temple at Tierra Grande.* He is also the author of two collections of short stories, *The Ghost of John Wayne* (University of Arizona, 2001) and *Circling the Tortilla Dragon* (Creative Arts, 2002), and a book of essays, *The Underground Heart* (Arizona, 2002). He is the editor of twelve anthologies, most recently *No Boundaries: Prose Poems by 24 American Poets* (Tupelo Press, 2003). He founded *LUNA,* a poetry journal, in 1998. His poetry has twice previously been selected for *The Best American Poetry:* by Robert Bly in 1999 and by Rita Dove in 2000. He is professor of English at the University of Minnesota.

Gonzalez writes: " 'Max Jacob's Shoes' was written to honor the resurgence of the prose poem in American poetry, but also to acknowledge one of its French masters who has often been overlooked in discussions of the genre. The prose poems in his book *The Dice Cup* appear to say that a poet can celebrate a dark vision as he unfolds his perceptions and gives them to an unsuspecting world. Jacob's attempts at artistic and personal survival resulted in prose poetry that allowed the poet to break out of the poem. He was able to free himself from what he wrote by confronting his demons and laughing at the plight of the visionary seeker in the company of such forces. Through sheer linguistic power, he took his being out of the text by acknowledging poetry as a celebration, a dance, and as a fleeing light beyond human limitations, even those that insist you have to wear shoes."

LINDA GREGG was born in Suffern, New York, in 1942. Her fifth book of poems, *Things and Flesh,* was published by Graywolf Press in 1999. Her first two books, *Too Bright to See* and *Alma,* were republished jointly by Graywolf Press in 2002. She currently lives in New York City and teaches at Princeton University.

Of "Beauty," Gregg writes: "This poem was born out of my memories of Brigitte Bardot when clandestine video footage of her was shown on *Entertainment Tonight.* She was lovely in her old films, but she no longer lives there. She has struggled to leave that fiction, to be real in her privacy. The world so often treats beauty harshly, especially at the end. Like the wilderness, the quiet, and the cities. We know women must protect their lives, but that's my point. She did."

MARK HALLIDAY was born in Ann Arbor, Michigan, in 1949. He teaches in the creative writing program at Ohio University. His books of poems are *Little Star* (William Morrow, 1987), *Tasker Street* (University of Massachusetts, 1992), *Selfwolf* (University of Chicago, 1999), and *JAB* (University of Chicago, 2002). His critical study, *Stevens and the Interpersonal,* was published by Princeton University Press in 1991.

Halliday writes: "Poetry is always about saying what can't be said— that beguiling hypnotic paradox. As a poet who usually places a high value on clarity and readability, I'm naturally troubled by the infinity of what my poems don't catch. In 'The Opaque' I experiment with dwelling in the gnarly otherness of what I haven't been able to interpret. But I find (humanly) that I can't live there."

MICHAEL S. HARPER was born in Brooklyn, New York, in 1938. He has taught at Brown University since 1970, and was named the first poet laureate of the state of Rhode Island. His most recent books of poetry are *Honorable Amendments* (1995) and *Songlines in Michaeltree* (1999), both from the University of Illinois. He is the co-editor of the anthologies *Every Shut Eye Ain't Asleep* (Little, Brown, 1994) and *The Vintage Anthology of African American Poetry* (Turtleback Books, 2000).

Of "Rhythmic Arrangements (on prosody)," Harper writes: "This exercise, in couplets, is an ars poetica and a steady reminder of ancestral kinship out of 'antagonistic cooperation'; it is a critique of the alexandrine; also an exercise in idioms and conceits; an inheritance; a ledger; a catechism; a poetics, perhaps a codicil of making by force out of confusion; also, a discourse on internal channeling; prayer; it is about race and gender, geography, caste and class, and count, which is a form of audiation, a scrupulous meanness out of Joyce, a lesson from the Bible, a vernacular tract of making out of force; cartography is mapmaking; the heart alive in the symmetry of mindless play."

MATTHEA HARVEY was born in Bad Homburg, Germany, in 1973. She is currently the poetry editor of *American Letters and Commentary* and teaches in the MFA program at Warren Wilson College. Her first book is *Pity the Bathtub Its Forced Embrace of the Human Form* (Alice James Books, 2001). Her second, *Sad Little Breathing Machine,* is forthcoming from Graywolf Press in Spring 2004. She lives in Brooklyn, New York.

Harvey writes: " 'Sad Little Breathing Machine' is the title poem of my second book and the first poem I wrote with an engine—a device I created to stymie my tendency toward narrative. The engines propel the poems on the level of subject, syntax, and imagery, but like a car engine they work mysteriously under the title's hood. The '@' sign in 'Sad Little Breathing Machine' signals the poem's subject of location and containment both through meaning and typographical appearance (i.e., the 'a' cradled in the '@' sign). The poem then progresses in a radial rather than linear manner, cataloging varieties of enclosure ranging from the invisible boundaries of the self to a cough in a tugboat."

GEORGE HIGGINS was born in Detroit, Michigan, in 1956. He received a B.A. from the University of Utah in 1977 and a J.D. from the University of Michigan Law School in 1980, where he studied briefly with Robert Hayden. After fifteen years in legal practice as a navy judge advocate and an Alameda County public defender, he returned to writing in 1995. He earned an MFA from Warren Wilson College in January 2002, where he was a Holden Scholar. He lives in Oakland, California, with his wife and two daughters, where he is still an assistant public defender. "Villanelle" is his first published poem.

Of "Villanelle," Higgins writes: "Perhaps the poem does nothing more than call to our attention this peculiar incident of the famous movie director who made an appearance at an inner city high school. Most recall the event because of what the school children did, but the subsequent media happening made a greater impression on me.

"My own children were (and still are) in the Oakland public schools. At the time I wrote the poem my wife, my daughter, and I were caught up in the struggle to improve or at least survive, possibly flourish, in the environment of our own school. In one of many such battles, we tried to get our school janitors to pick up the garbage that flowed out of the playground cans and rotted on the blacktop. In a scene reminiscent of *Bleak House,* I remember my wife taking posed Polaroids of smiling school children standing next to garbage week after week in an effort to build a case against the janitors. There was something about the ugliness we witnessed that made the appearance of Steven Spielberg seem almost magical by its contrast, even if the magic was short-lived. This may be why the refrain in the first line of the poem occurred to me one winter evening in my dorm room at Warren Wilson College in North Carolina. Oh, by the way, Mr. Spielberg actually visited Castlemont High School, which I could not get to scan or rhyme properly."

EDWARD HIRSCH was born in Chicago, Illinois, in 1950. He has published six books of poems with Knopf: *For the Sleepwalkers* (1981); *Wild Gratitude* (1986), which won the National Book Critics Circle Award; *The Night Parade* (1989); *Earthly Measures* (1994); *On Love* (1998); and *Lay Back the Darkness* (2003). He has also written three prose books: *How to Read a Poem and Fall in Love with Poetry* (Harcourt, 1999), a national bestseller; *Responsive Reading* (University of Michigan Press, 1999); and *The Demon and the Angel: Searching for the Source of Artistic Inspiration* (Harcourt, 2002). He writes the weekly Poet's Choice column in the *Washington Post Book World.* He has received the Prix de Rome, a Guggenheim Fellowship, an American Academy of Arts and Letters Award for Literature, and a MacArthur Fellowship. After teaching in the creative writing program at the University of Houston for seventeen years, he recently became the fourth president of the John Simon Guggenheim Memorial Foundation, which was founded in 1925.

Hirsch writes: " 'The Desire Manuscripts' is a sequence of seven poems. I feel a tension in the title—*Desire* takes us in one direction, *Manuscripts* in another. In each poem—the first five are sonnets—a lover addresses his beloved through the scrim of a classic text. This enabled me to explore my own passions through encounters with key moments in poetry, ground books that have meant a great deal to me. In 'The Sentence,' for example—a one-sentence terza rima sonnet—Canto Five of Dante's *Inferno* is brought into the bedroom. In 'The Mourning Fields'— a three-sentence terza rima sonnet—it is Book Six of Virgil's *Aeneid* that haunts the speaker while his lover sleeps beside him.

"Most of these are underworld poems. The last two, each one sentence long, refer to the Orpheus story, which is, after all, the *ur*-poetic tale. There is a whole body of Orphic texts that were lost to us, and in the last poem I invent one of them (*The Lost Orphics*) to tell a bedrock story and try to create a poignancy of loss and regret.

"One premise of this sequence of desire is that great poems deliver us to ourselves. They read us."

TONY HOAGLAND was born in a U.S. Army base hospital in North Carolina in 1953. He has published two collections of poetry: *Sweet Ruin* (University of Wisconsin Press, 1992) and *Donkey Gospel* (Graywolf Press, 1998). A third collection, *What Narcissism Means to Me,* will be published by Graywolf in fall 2003. A book of essays is also forthcoming.

Of "Summer Night," Hoagland writes: "Here's a lyric summer poem. I've always been terrified of the price tag of domesticity, the way marriage, or its equivalents, can shrink, rather than expand the heart and mind. You know that, after a fight, Adam and Eve might as well have been in downtown Cleveland as in the Garden of Eden. 'What's that, a nightingale?—well, it's ugly, and I wish it would shut up.'

"So the poem is about the mixed impulses of compassion and cruelty, defense and empathy, blindness and attention, which are so much a part of walking around human. Those fractions, those numerators and dividends, are tonally embodied in the details. If the human part of the story is all too familiar, the hero is nature, which keeps showing up, trying to redeem the situation, begging for a piece of our attention before it's too late."

RICHARD HOWARD was born in Cleveland, Ohio, in 1929. He was educated at Columbia University and the Sorbonne. The most recent of his twelve books of poems is *Talking Cures* (Turtle Point Press, 2002). For his third, *Untitled Subjects,* he was awarded the Pulitzer Prize in 1970. He has translated more than 150 works from the French, including Stendhal's *The Charterhouse of Parma* for the Modern Library and Baudelaire's *Les Fleurs du mal,* which received the American Book Award. He served as the poet laureate of New York State from 1994 to 1995. In 1996 he was named a fellow of the MacArthur Foundation and is currently poetry editor of both *The Paris Review* and *Western Humanities Review.* He teaches in the writing division of the School of the Arts at Columbia University and was the guest editor of *The Best American Poetry 1995.*

Of "Success," Howard writes: "One is frequently asked, regarding poems like this, 'Did you make that up?' To which I should like to answer: I made up the poem; Alice Neel was real; life is imaginary."

RODNEY JONES was born in Hartselle, Alabama, in 1950. He is the author of eight books of poetry: *Going Ahead, Looking Back* (Southbound Books, 1977); *The Story They Told Us of Light* (University of Alabama Press, 1980); *The Unborn* (The Atlantic Monthly Press, 1985); and *Transparent Gestures* (1989), *Apocalyptic Narrative* (1993), *Things That Happen Once* (1996), *Elegy for the Southern Drawl* (1999), and *Kingdom of the Instant* (2002), all from Houghton Mifflin. He lives with his family in Carbondale, Illinois, and teaches at Southern Illinois University.

Jones writes: " 'Ten Sighs' was fun to write, no big ideas, just going down the slide in my journal, but something of the spirit of Roethke came into play, and it seemed true enough, so I hung on to it and worked. The great man in part five is Allen Tate, my teacher for a few weeks, who was no doubt waxing poetical when he said that he loathed and detested poetry."

JOY KATZ was born in Newark, New Jersey, in 1963. She was educated at Ohio State, Washington University in St. Louis, and Stanford, where she held a Wallace Stegner Fellowship. Her first book, *Fabulae,* was published by Southern Illinois University Press in 2002. She is co-editor of the forthcoming anthology *Dark Horses: Poets on Overlooked Poems.* Trained in industrial design, she works in New York City as a designer and editor.

Katz writes: "Entering history can be an intimate process. Public events become embedded in our lives, like slivers lodged under fingernails—a friend remembers my age because I was born the year President

Kennedy was shot. 'Some Rain' began as a log of the time of day and the weather conditions for various historic events. It was two hundred lines long. After many drafts, and after many months, there was just rain."

BRIGIT PEGEEN KELLY was born in Palo Alto, California, in 1951. She has published two books of poetry, *To the Place of Trumpets* (Yale University Press, 1988) and *Song* (BOA Editions, Ltd., 1995). A third collection of poems is forthcoming from BOA in 2004. She teaches in the creative writing program at the University of Illinois at Urbana-Champaign.

Of "The Dragon," Kelly writes: "It's funny, my memory of writing this poem doesn't seem to line up with the drafts I saved. I don't know what that means. But I do know this. Originally, I felt I had to frame the material that now comprises the poem. Probably the most significant aspect of the revision process involved letting go of the elaborate frame I had constructed."

GALWAY KINNELL was born in Providence, Rhode Island, in 1927. He is Erich Maria Remarque Professor of Creative Writing at New York University. His latest book of poetry is *A New Selected Poems* (Houghton Mifflin, 2001).

Of "When the Towers Fell," Kinnell asks the reader to note that printed in italics are passages quoted from *The Testament*, by François Villon; "For the Marriage of Faustus and Helen," by Hart Crane; "Death Fugue," by Paul Celan; "Songs of a Wanderer," by Aleksander Wat; "City of Ships" and "When Lilacs Last in the Door-yard Bloom'd," by Walt Whitman. The passages which are in languages other than English are roughly translated as follows:

> . . . poor and rich
> Wise and foolish, priests and laymen,
> Noblemen, serfs, generous and mean,
> Short and tall and handsome and homely . . .
>   —François Villon

> Black milk of daybreak we drink it at evening
> we drink it at midday and morning we drink it at night
> we drink it and drink it
> *   *   *
> we're digging a grave in the sky there'll be plenty of room
> to lie down there
>   —Paul Celan

> They do not become, they are.
> Nothing but that, I thought,
> Now loathing within myself
> Everything that becomes.
> —Aleksander Wat

CAROLYN KIZER was born in Spokane, Washington, on December 10 (Emily Dickinson's birthday) in 1925. Her first published poem appeared in *The New Yorker* when she was a seventeen-year-old student at Sarah Lawrence College. Her first book of poems, *The Ungrateful Garden,* was published by Indiana University Press in 1961; Doubleday published the next two, *Knock upon Silence* (1965) and *Midnight Was My Cry* (1971). She received the 1985 Pulitzer Prize for *Yin* (BOA Editions). All of her other books of poetry have been published by Copper Canyon: *Mermaids in the Basement* (1984), *The Nearness of You* (1986), *Harping On* (1996), and *Cool, Calm, and Collected* (2001). She has also published several books of criticism and edited the anthology *100 Great Poems by Women* (Ecco, 1995).

Of "After Horace," Kizer writes: "I will always be grateful to J. D. McClatchy for offering me the chance to 'translate' this Ode 1.13 of Horace, among others. Having had a spotty, 'un-classical' education, I relished this glimpse of an author and a language unknown to me. This ode, I feel, is the most successful one that I tried because first of all it is a *poem.* I was happy that the editor of *Poetry* agreed with me.

"I have always felt comfortable with the cloak of another poet's identity. We poets have that in common with fine actors: it's both the fun of masquerading and the occasional need to hide behind someone else. Also, it is a relief from the anxiety of drying up—more important than the 'anxiety of influence'!"

JENNIFER L. KNOX was born in 1968 in Lancaster, California, where a young Frank Zappa led the high school band, and Captain Beefheart lived across the street from the headquarters of the Flat Earth Society. She received her MFA from New York University, and currently teaches at Hunter College while moonlighting as the art director of the National Arts Club in New York City. Her work has appeared in *The Best American Poetry 1997* and *Great American Prose Poems: From Poe to the Present.* She is at work on her first book, *A Gringo Like Me.* She lives in Brooklyn with a husband, writer Sean McNally, and a cat, Tokyo Roy.

Of "Love Blooms at Chimsbury After the War," Knox writes: "I was at a reading, listening to a young woman whose story was set in World War II England, and she was reading it with this fancy windswept Joan Collins kind of British accent, and every time I tuned back in, another character seemed to be dropping dead of tuberculosis. I don't know what else happened in the story, but it was incredible, and went on for thirty-five minutes. I knew that I wanted to replicate it, but I didn't know where to start. Weeks later I went to hear poet Marie Ponsot read, and after a poem called 'Winter,' she began a sentence about 'That particular sonnet...' I couldn't believe it: '*That* was fourteen lines long?' I hardly ever write in form, but it was the key to the poem. People can't just go around dropping dead all over the place for as long as they feel like it—there needs to be rules, or at least an end in sight."

KENNETH KOCH was born in Cincinnati, Ohio, in 1925. After serving in the United States Army in World War II, seeing action as a rifleman in the Philippines, he went to Harvard on the GI Bill. Following graduation in 1948, he moved to New York City, where he became a central figure of the New York School of Poetry. He received his doctorate at Columbia University and taught there for forty years. His course in imaginative writing proved a college highlight for many future writers. *Ko, or A Season on Earth,* a long poem in ottava rima, appeared in 1960; *Thank You and Other Poems* followed two years later. He adapted his teaching techniques to the needs of elementary school children and elderly residents of nursing homes, and worked a minor revolution in pedagogy through such influential books as *Rose, Where Did You Get That Red?* (1973) and *I Never Told Anybody* (1977). His recent collections of poetry include *On the Great Atlantic Rainway: Selected Poems 1950–1988* (1994), *One Train* (1994), *Straits* (1998), *New Addresses* (2000), and the posthumous *A Possible World* (2002), all from Knopf. Also published in the 1990s were two books about poetry: *The Art of Poetry* (University of Michigan, 1996) and *Making Your Own Days* (Scribner, 1998).

"When I first read his poems I felt as though I had been standing for a very long time and that someone had just pushed a big comfortable chair behind me for me to sit in, where I could relax and take notes on what was going on around me," John Ashbery said, introducing Koch at a poetry reading in the 1960s. "In other words I feel his poems give the world back to you; you always had it but somehow from reading works of literature you felt that there must be some difference between it and what you thought it was, with what your experience offered up to you, which always seems like such a miserable thing in comparison with what everybody else has." At another New York reading from that era, Ashbery quoted three lines from his friend's poem "Lunch": "Do you see that snowman tackled over there / By summer and the sea? The boardwalk went to Istanbul / And back under his left eye." Ashbery commented, "This seems at first to be a random enumeration of impossible relationships and events. But all poetry contains these, a fact the lines casually remind us of as they are hurrying to make their point, which is that all kinds of fantastic and dull exchanges are going on in the air around us all the time, that the world is a wonderful and horrible place, that we are all existing at a very fast pace, that things like love and death and old age and platonic love are important things and full of interest. The final result of Koch's releasing so much hitherto classified information, which we already knew without being able to experience it, is a new kind of energy that is very real and precious, which will stimulate anyone who lets himself come in contact with it."

Kenneth Koch died in July 2002.

JOHN KOETHE was born in San Diego, California, on Christmas Day, 1945. He is the author of six books of poetry, most recently *Falling Water* (1997), which received the Kingsley Tufts Award; *The Constructor* (1999); and *North Point North: New and Selected Poems* (2002), all from HarperCollins. He is also the author of *The Continuity of Wittgenstein's Thought* (Cornell University Press, 1996) and *Poetry at One Remove: Essays* (University of Michigan Press, 2000). He is Distinguished Professor of Philosophy at the University of Wisconsin-Milwaukee.

Koethe writes: " 'Y2K (1933)' is a somewhat paranoid and vaguely political poem I wrote after reading a review of a book about Nazi Germany that described a phenomenon called 'working towards the Führer.' The idea was that middle-level functionaries were supposed to intuit Hitler's wishes and intentions and design policies to implement them without being explicitly ordered to do so. It seemed to me to have an air of anonymous menace about it, and I decided to work the phrase into a poem that would share that air."

TED KOOSER was born in Ames, Iowa, in 1939. A retired life insurance executive, he lives near the village of Garland, Nebraska, and teaches as a visiting professor at the University of Nebraska. He has published eight collections of poetry, the most recent being *Braided Creek* (Copper Canyon, 2003), which is a conversation in short poems with poet and novelist Jim Harrison. He is also the author of *Local Wonders: Seasons in the Bohemian Alps* (University of Nebraska Press, 2002), a seasonal memoir.

Kooser writes: "The University of Nebraska State Museum in Lincoln, Nebraska, is next door to Andrews Hall, home of the English Department. When I need a short break from meeting students, I sometimes take a solitary walk through the museum's collections, which include a number of skeletons of mastodons and other ancient creatures. My poem 'In the Hall of Bones' is set in that museum, where it is so quiet in midafternoon that one's feet clip-clop over the stone floors like the ghostly hooves of something we once were."

PHILIP LEVINE was born in Detroit, Michigan, in 1928. He presently teaches one course a year at New York University and divides his time between Fresno, California, and Brooklyn, New York. His most recent book of poems is *The Mercy* (Knopf, 1999). In 2002 the University of Michigan Press published two of his prose works: *So Ask: Essay and Conversations* and a paperback edition of *The Bread of Time: Toward an Autobiography*.

Of "The Music of Time," Levine writes: "A few years ago I saw the movie 'The Buena Vista Social Club,' & it brought back the Havana I'd known one summer fifty years before. There were the same cars looking a little more tired, the same buildings a little shabbier, & the same music I'd heard on the streets—perhaps played & sung by the same people. My strongest memory is of the room I stayed in on Calle Obisbo; it was large & looked larger than it was because almost nothing was in it; the floors, which were deliciously cool, might actually have been marble, for the building had been a classy 'family' hotel decades earlier. Above the bed was a large, ornate fan that took its time. If I hadn't been me I might have been in a John Houston movie. The French doors opened onto a tiny balcony with a view of a room no more than a dozen feet away in which a group of young women & girls were continually sewing, & one—the eldest—seemed always to be singing, perhaps to herself, perhaps to the girls, perhaps to the world. Every morning when I wakened I would wash my face, brush my teeth, & go out on the balcony, & the women & the girls would greet me with 'Buenas Dias' & then with songs. I tried to capture that joyous gift in a lonely time, but another series of nightly walks intruded & darkened the poem: those taken years later in the old working class barrio of Barcelona during the terrible Franco years."

J. D. MCCLATCHY was born in Bryn Mawr, Pennsylvania, in 1945. He lives in New York City and in Stonington, Connecticut, and is a professor of English at Yale University and a chancellor of the Academy of American Poets. He has written five books of poems: *Scenes from Another Life* (Braziller, 1981), *Stars Principal* (Macmillan, 1986), *The Rest of the Way* (Knopf, 1990), *Ten Commandments* (Knopf, 1998), and *Hazmat* (Knopf, 2002). His selected poems, *Division of Spoils,* was published in England by Arc in 2003. Two collections of his essays have appeared: *White Paper* (1989) and *Twenty Questions* (1998), both from Columbia University Press. In addition, he has written four opera libretti and edited many books, including *Horace: The Odes* (Princeton, 2002) and Edna St. Vincent Millay's *Selected Poems* (Library of America, 2003). He is editor of *The Yale Review* and the Random House AudioBooks series The Voice of the Poet.

Of "Jihad," McClatchy writes: "I have a long-standing interest in Arab culture and history, as several poems in earlier collections of mine will testify. I had written this poem long before September 11, 2001, interested less in the morality of the situation than in the psychology that prompts it. Each sonnet's italicized sestet is a pastiche of the Koran, and might either have been spoken by the mullah mentioned in the last stanza, or have been echoing in the mind of the fanatic in the last stanza.

"After the terrorist attack on the World Trade Center, the editors of the op-ed page of the *New York Times* learned of my poem, as yet unpublished, and telephoned to ask me if they could run it. I agreed on the condition that they allow me to append a note explaining that the poem was not written in response to 9/11. They agreed, and I hurriedly wrote the note, expanding the facts to include a short meditation on the fraught relationship between poetry and history. The *Times* called to thank me and said they'd run the facts, not the meditation.

"A day passed, and then they called again—this time to say their editorial board had wrangled and had finally decided they would *not* be running the poem. When I asked why, I was told they feared it might offend the Palestinians. I burst out laughing. I had thought, after all, that was the point of pieces on the op-ed page. And what do I think now? Feelings were running high at the time, the *Times* was nervous about implications and reactions. As it happens, I'm in favor of the Palestinian cause. But poems aren't platforms. A poet—as distinct from other, perhaps more persuasive, kinds of writers—can only unstitch the weave of tangled threads in order to pattern them anew as an alternative picture of events. Poems are meant to complicate our sense of things, not stroke them. In this poem, I had wanted to look at things not from the victims' side or the dazed teenaged bomber's, but, as it were, from as remote a point of view as scripture's."

W. S. MERWIN was born in New York City in 1927 and has also lived in Spain, England, France, Mexico, and Hawaii. For many years, he kept an apartment in the West Village, on Seventh Avenue, from which he watched the World Trade Center being built. His most recent books include *The Pupil* (2001), a translation of Dante's *Purgatorio* (2000), and *The River Sound* (1999), all from Knopf. Copper Canyon Press also published *Flower & Hand* (1997) and *East Window* (1999), translations of Asian poetry. A book of prose—part memoir, part history—entitled *The Mays of Ventadorn* (National Geographic Books) was published in 2002. He has received the Pulitzer Prize (for *The Carrier of Ladders*), the PEN Translation Prize, the Dorothea Tanning Prize from the Academy of American Poets, and a writer's award from the Lila Wallace–Reader's Digest Fund.

Of "To Zbigniew Herbert's Bicycle," Merwin writes: "I knew Zbigniew Herbert for many years, though we saw each other rarely. In the weeks after September 11, 2001, a number of poems came, with connections to the event that were obvious to me, at least. Then one morning I woke knowing that I wanted to write this poem, and in the course of the day this is how it turned out. I knew I had been greatly saddened by Zbigniew's death. I certainly knew nothing about his ever having had a bicycle. But this poem seemed to me to belong with the poems written in the wake of that other shock and sorrow."

HEATHER MOSS lives in Baltimore, where she was born in 1973. She earns a living as an acquisitions technician in an academic library. She attended the University of Montana and attributes her passion for literature and writing to its department of English and to the extraordinary parenting skills of her mother. "Dear Alter Ego" is her first publication.

Of "Dear Alter Ego," Moss writes: "When I wrote this, I was thinking about love and religion, two institutions that have the capacity to produce a legion of physical relics. Sometimes it's hard to ascertain where the human being ends and the relics begin, especially for the person in question. As I am a hopeless packrat, I wondered what it might be like to divest a part of one's self and the corresponding objects."

STANLEY MOSS was born in New York City in 1926. He attended Trinity College and Yale University. He makes his living as a private Old Master picture dealer, specializing in Spanish and Italian painting. He is the editor and publisher of Sheep Meadow Press. *A History of Color: New and Collected Poems* was recently published by Seven Stories Press.

Of "A History of Color," Moss writes: "I was taken by the colors of everyday clouds, which led me to my secret life with color, in erogenous zones, language, religion, the arts—call it the history of color. Early on in the poem it became clear that if color were the protagonist, death was the antagonist. I attacked him with the means at hand: peppermints, insults, whatever. I have some lingering affection for a mountain of material discarded: the cloth and jewelry in biblical dress; Goethe's book on color, which he thought more important than *Faust;* the fact that science tells us we don't see color at all, that all colors are nothing more than magnetic waves that we process into color in the brain; and so on."

PAUL MULDOON was born in Northern Ireland in 1951 and is now a citizen of the United States. His most recent books are *Poems 1968–1998* (2001) and *Moy Sand and Gravel* (2002), both from Farrar, Straus and Giroux. He teaches at Princeton University. He received the Pulitzer Prize for poetry in 2003.

Muldoon writes: " 'The Loaf' is set in a house on the bank of the Delaware and Raritan Canal, a canal built in the 1830s by Irishmen, many of whom were lost to cholera, many more to the severity of their lives."

PEGGY MUNSON was born in Normal, Illinois, in 1968. Educated at Oberlin College, where she received a degree in creative writing in 1991, she is the editor of *Stricken: Voices from the Hidden Epidemic of Chronic Fatigue Syndrome* (Haworth Press, 2000). She lives in Providence, Rhode Island.

Of "Four Deaths That Happened Daily," Munson writes: "This poem—like most of my poems—is a staged car wreck that never happens. It tries to deal with the reconciliation of opposites. Hope Street is one of the longest streets in Providence and people like to say here: 'Most of us live off Hope.' Hope snakes through the city to become another street without signage. One night, horribly sick with chronic illness and half wondering if I should end it, I drove down Hope and recklessly ran a red light. I had never played chicken with myself like that and it felt thrilling, but I wanted to feel more alive, not dead. There is a beautiful flirtation that happens with death sometimes when one is healthy and able; it's quite another thing when death itself feels familial, an annoying aunt who clucks her tongue and points to the clock. That night, I felt a numbness that made me crave horses in guns. I wanted to feel the rearing life instinct masked as death, García Lorca's *duende*. But the guns were not what I thought. Destructive, yes, but I wasn't seeking their literal end: I was seeking transformational power over daily deaths, which felt physical, emotional, esoteric, many things. I was trying to accept that Hope was just a street.

"The poetic form is an accident that is only unconsciously intentional, and that is its beauty. Since I wondered if the obsessive quest for meaning and structure stops people from living, I wanted the poem to demand transparency. Does daily death come from our inability to transform dictatorial iconography of Freud (analysis), Rorschach (assumed perception), Swastika (evil), Apartheid (sadistic separation)? Can these things ever be reduced to innocuous meanings; i.e., can a dismantled Apartheid ever go back to its literal meaning of 'separation' and encompass truth? Can we see contrast, feel the faction of bodies all the way down to the eyelash, and still embrace an abstract sense of connection and completeness? Does our wait for the abolitionists of light and shadow keep us from embracing wholeness? Sometimes, a gun cannot be a literal gun, or we can't go on."

MARILYN NELSON was born in Cleveland, Ohio, in 1946. Her publications include *For the Body* (1978), *Mama's Promises* (1985), *The Homeplace* (1990), *Magnificat* (1994), and *The Fields of Praise: New and Selected Poems* (1997), all published by LSU Press, and *Carver: A Life in Poems* (2001), published by Front Street Books. Her rendition of Euripides' play *Hecuba* appears in *Euripides I,* the first volume of the Penn Greek Drama Series. She has received fellowships from the Guggenheim Foundation and twice from the National Endowment for the Arts. A professor of English at the University of Delaware, she is poet laureate of the state of Connecticut.

Of "Asparagus," Nelson writes: "This sonnet, one of a longer sequence, presents a simple and delicious recipe and instructions for eating asparagus in a way that turns a dinner party into a scene from *Tom Jones.* The speaker of the poem is a young wife whose husband is having an affair."

DANIEL NESTER was born in Portsmouth, Virginia, in 1968. He grew up in Maple Shade, New Jersey, and was educated at Rutgers University's Camden campus and New York University (MFA, 1997). He is the author of *God Save My Queen* (Soft Skull Press, 2003), a meditation on his obsession with the British rock band Queen. He is also the editor of the online journal *Unpleasant Event Schedule* (unpleasanteventschedule.com), the former editor of *La Petite Zine,* and a contributing editor to *Painted Bride Quarterly.* A teacher and technical writer, he lives in the Park Slope section of Brooklyn with his wife, Maisie Weissman.

Of "Poem for the Novelist Whom I Forced to Write a Poem," Nester writes: "The poem was written at the Virginia Center for the Creative Arts, where I was enduring a writing block. I confessed this to Christina Askounis, a novelist at an adjacent studio, and it turned out that she was similarly afflicted. One night, we both fell in love with a poem by the East German poet Ulrich Berkes called 'Exaggerated Self-Portrait,' which I found in an old *Paris Review* from 1988. It's a list of personal details that is precise and wonderful. We decided to write our own versions of the poem as an exercise, and before Christina went home weeks later, she dropped off hers in a business envelope.

"It just blew me away. There was everyday detail, guilty pleasures, God, boxing. For inspiration she was looking at her own experience rather than 'the birds at the feeder.' To me, her poem was a real attempt at 'Personism,' Frank O'Hara's idea of putting poems 'squarely between the poet and the person.' This explains my purposefully ham-handed allusion to his great poem 'Why I Am Not a Painter.' So I'm writing a poem-letter to this novelist as well as soapboxing my own *ars poetica.*"

NAOMI SHIHAB NYE was born in St. Louis, Missouri, in 1952. Her recent books include *19 Varieties of Gazelle: Poems of the Middle East* (HarperCollins, 2002); *Come with Me: Poems for a Journey* (Greenwillow, 2000); *Fuel* (BOA Editions, 1998); and *Habibi* (Pocket Books, 1999), a novel for teens. She has edited seven prize-winning anthologies of poetry for young readers, including *This Same Sky* (Aladdin, 1996), *The Tree Is Older Than You Are* (Aladdin, 1998), *The Space Between Our Footsteps: Poems & Paintings from the Middle East* (Simon and Schuster, 1998), *What Have You Lost?* (Greenwillow, 2001), and *Salting the Ocean* (Greenwillow, 2000). She was named a Lannan Fellow for 2003. She lives in San Antonio, Texas.

Of "What Happened to Everybody," Nye writes: "Even as a very small child, I was seared by nostalgia, wondering where everything prior to our own lives had gone and where everything we saw and loved right then would *go*. Standing on the front porch in the softening twilight, washed by the dissolving waves of the day, I would weep for this ancient mystery of time. Anyone who found me there thought I had been stung by bees or was a totally wasted weirdo (my brother's frequent impression), but I knew my sorrow was founded in something that would haunt me for the rest of my days. So the fact that the neighborhood in which we lived then appears virtually unchanged today (all the same old houses, our same historical redbrick school, the same little green park in which we played still studded with evening cries and the bounce of the ball) is curious and compelling. Of course, the people have changed. Integration happened, thank goodness. But so much still appears to be right in place. Perhaps I was haunted by loss since my father was a Palestinian refugee who had 'lost everything.' However, his life of family and culture and memory and two languages seemed richer than anyone else's life that I could see. I guess I have been writing about this basic mystery of loss and change forever; it is an ongoing topic and will never be 'solved' but only approached, gingerly and tenderly, with sorrow and care."

ISHLE YI PARK was born in 1977 and raised in Queens, New York. She works as writer-in-residence at the Youth Speaks Literary Arts Center in San Francisco. Her first book, *The Temperature of This Water,* will be released by Kaya Press this year.

Park writes: "Queen Min Bi was the last empress of Korea. I visited her birthplace in Yuju, Korea, where there is a museum dedicated to her memory, and it inspired the writing of this poem."

ROBERT PINSKY was born in Long Branch, New Jersey, in 1940. He is the author of six books of poems, most recently, *Jersey Rain* (Farrar, Straus and Giroux, 2000), and translator of *The Inferno of Dante.* As United States Poet Laureate he started the Favorite Poem Project, and he continues his work on this audio and video archive featuring Americans from all walks of life reading aloud beloved poems. He is the poetry editor of *Slate* magazine and a regular contributor to *The NewsHour with Jim Lehrer* on PBS. He teaches in the graduate writing program at Boston University.

Of "Anniversary," Pinsky writes: "The *Washington Post* commissioned this poem. Their request was precise: the editors wanted a poem not about the September 11 attacks but about the year that followed that day. They invited me to interpret the assignment however I chose.

"A natural response for the reader might be, 'That was a hard assignment'—but no: every work of art deals with a hard assignment. Any poem worth writing wrestles with its own impossibility.

"Difficulties are materials.

"The weight given to the specific date. The way the date seems to have become a word. The perhaps inevitable media exploitation, with the music business and the television business and the print business all performing in ways that seemed sometimes awful and sometimes admirable, and the two often impossible to tell apart. The true American spirit always a little crazier, more ambiguous, more enigmatic than any version of it. The old question of who we think we are, presented in a terrible new way. These interested me.

"I wanted to acknowledge that what happened did in some sense happen to all of us, yet I did not want to cooperate with the Bush administration's use of that shared feeling. I wanted to acknowledge that some people had performed heroically, yet I did not feel easy with the word 'hero.' I wanted to avoid jingoism, but I wanted to express my loyalty to our modern, secular world as a living thing, an organism including not only its ideals of human rights, the liberation of women and so forth, but its vulgarity and eccentricity and excess. (Though I would never call the Rayettes or Katherine Lee Bates 'vulgar'!) I wanted to apprehend the magnitude of the event, yet I was aware that dimensions evolve gradually, over years; in that regard I was grateful for the terms of the assignment: the concentration not on the event but on the time since the event. The year."

KEVIN PRUFER was born in Cleveland, Ohio, in 1969, and now lives in Warrensburg, Missouri. His newest book is *The Finger Bone* (Carnegie Mellon University Press, 2002). He is editor of *Pleiades: A Journal of New Writing* and *The New Young American Poets* (Southern Illinois University Press, 2000).

Of "What the Paymaster Said," Prufer writes: "I worked as an office temp in St. Louis while I was in graduate school. Because I could type pretty well and was competent with computers, I got easy jobs that paid nicely. I typed letters for a company that designed thermostats for manufacture by low-paid workers in Mexico. I worked for an insurance office where all day long I could hear over the cubicle walls bored telephone operators explaining to sick policyholders why their prescriptions weren't covered. I even spent a summer in a bank department that handled accounts of only the very rich. I'd show up every morning in my jacket and tie and, if there was work to be done, I'd do it. If not, I'd surf the Internet, read newspapers, or write poems.

"One day, I happened to read an article in the Kansas City *Star* about a terrible economic depression in a country that, at the time, I couldn't even find on a map. The currency in that country was so worthless that factory owners were offering to pay employees in lengths of wood or bags of food. The article was short—only a paragraph—wedged between a couple of gossipy little pieces about movie stars.

"About a year later, I wrote 'What the Paymaster Said.' The paymaster's is the voice of authority: commanding, insinuating, and desperate that the employee just behave."

ED ROBERSON was born in Pittsburgh, Pennsylvania, in 1939. He is the author of *When Thy King Is a Boy* (University of Pittsburgh Press, 1970); *Etai-Eken* (University of Pittsburgh Press, 1975); *Lucid Interval as Integral Music* (Harmattan Press, 1985); *Voices Cast Out to Talk Us In* (University of Iowa Press, 1995); *Just In/Word of Navigational Challenges: New and Selected Work* (Talisman House Press, 1998); and *Atmosphere Conditions* (Sun and Moon Press, 2000). He has received a Lila Wallace–Reader's Digest Writer's Award.

Roberson writes: " 'Sequoia sempervirens' is from a series of poems about our cities. It questions what humans are about by a rhetorical argument in comparisons. These trees live up to 2,200 years. I wanted to construct comparisons that were as beyond proportion as their reality, outrageous, strutting comparisons because humans like to have everything measured against themselves. A simple ratio such as 'five cat years to one human year' doesn't put us in our place, so the poem in the plain speech of numbers that first came to mind wouldn't work.

"Because these trees grow to over 350 feet, they are living lightning rods; the forests are constantly struck and set afire. When you consider the number of major storms per year and the fact that these forests experience a major forest fire every forty years, these trees appear to live in fire like we live in rain—or like many human cities appear to constantly grow within and out of their own fires of ruin.

"These are the thoughts that give rise to the closing images, but this layering appears near the beginning of the poem as an equation: 'foot totals map,' the measurements of the *foot* can *total* into a *map;* or those accumulations, *foot totals,* can *map* (now a verb) impossible cities layered on top of cities, upwards or down into histories. The poem is written for just such a layering in fragment.

"In the end, the spirit of the transitory, of the guest, blesses those who welcome it."

VIJAY SESHADRI was born in India in 1954 and came to the United States at the age of five. He grew up in Columbus, Ohio, attended Oberlin College, and has lived in many parts of the country, including the Oregon coast, where he spent five years working in the fishing and logging industries. He is the author of *Wild Kingdom* (Graywolf, 1996), a book of poems, and many essays and reviews. He teaches poetry and nonfiction writing at Sarah Lawrence College.

Seshadri writes: "Crucial to the architecture of 'The Disappearances' is a cataclysmic historical event, which the poem rises toward and manages to leave behind. I have vexed many times the problem of dealing with history vertically, rather than horizontally, which is the way we usually deal with it and which is why we as a species have the dreadful problems we have."

ALAN SHAPIRO was born in Boston, Massachusetts, in 1952. He is currently the William R. Kenan, Jr., Distinguished Professor of English as the University of North Carolina. He has published eight books of poetry, most recently *Mixed Company* (University of Chicago, 1996), winner of the *Los Angeles Times* Book Prize; *The Dead Alive and Busy* (University of Chicago, 2000), winner of the Kingsley Tufts Award; and *Song and Dance* (Houghton Mifflin, 2002). His memoir, *The Last Happy Occasion,* appeared from the University of Chicago in 1996. Oxford University Press will publish his translation of the *Oresteia* by Aeschylus in 2003. He lives in Hillsborough, North Carolina, with his son, Nat, and his daughter, Isabel.

Of "Sleet," Shapiro writes: "There are two voices in this poem, one voice asking what it feels like to be told by a doctor that your brother is going to die from an incurable form of cancer, and another more internal voice that answers by way of a childhood memory, a memory that is also a metaphor for what the speaker feels."

MYRA SHAPIRO, born in the Bronx in 1932, returned to New York after forty-five years in Georgia and Tennessee, where she married, raised two daughters, and worked as a librarian and a teacher of English. She teaches poetry workshops for the International Women's Writing Guild and serves on the board of directors of Poets House in New York City. Her book of poems, *I'll See You Thursday,* was published by Blue Sofa Press in 1996, and she has just completed a memoir, *Four Sublets: Becoming a Poet in New York.* Her work appeared in *The Best American Poetry 1999.* In 2003 she and her husband celebrate their fiftieth wedding anniversary.

Of "For Nazim Hikmet in the Old Prison, Now a Four Seasons Hotel," Shapiro writes: "When the taxi driver in Istanbul asked my destination and I said the Four Seasons, he didn't know where to go. Only after I told him it was a new hotel, in the Sultahnamet section of town, did his face light in recognition: 'Oh, the old prison.'

"I'd flown to Istanbul from New York; I was excited to be meeting my husband coming from Israel. It was our anniversary. On the flight I'd read Nazim Hikmet's poems translated by Randy Blasing and Mutlu Konuk, so I was aware of his years in jail as a political prisoner (as a Communist). At the hotel with its marble bathrooms and carpeted halls where there are still prisoners' words incised on pillars, I couldn't stop hearing his loving voice. That first night when I couldn't sleep, I wrote. Grateful for my life, grateful for poetry whose images can hold agony and joy in the same focus, I put my words beside Hikmet's telling me to celebrate."

BRUCE SMITH was born in Philadelphia, Pennsylvania, in 1946. He is the author of four books of poems: *The Common Wages* (Sheep Meadow, 1985), *Silver and Information* (National Poetry Series, University of Georgia, 1987), *Mercy Seat* (University of Chicago, 1994), and *The Other Lover* (University of Chicago, 2000), a finalist for both the National Book Award and the Pulitzer Prize. He teaches in the MFA program at Syracuse University.

Smith writes: " 'Song with a Child's Pacifier in It' is a poem in two voices. There is a song and a counter-song. A call and a response. A duet. The reader may read the poem as two poems—one poem made up of all the justified lines of the left margin and the other poem as all the indented lines. Or the reader may choose to read the poem as one piece whose music and movement is antiphonal. One line launches out and one hesitates, reconsiders, or launches out in its own direction. One signs; the other has a story to tell. One voice leads, the other follows— backwards and in high heels as they said of Ginger Rogers dancing with Fred Astaire. If there's a self, there's also a soul. The poem is of two minds. A yoking of history and ecstasy, haiku and hysteria, the text and its gloss, the lie and the truth. The poem read this way is interrupted— but what is not?—so it is partial, but with an abundance of partiality. The groove and the break. The tune and the improvisation. Trembling and transversing. Making (mastery) and receiving (mystery). Purpose and accident. Not just binaries—statement and contradiction—but the shuffling of the voices and the dealing out of . . . what? A third thing in the unrealized possibilities of the other two."

CHARLIE SMITH was born in 1947 in Moultrie, Georgia, raised there and educated variously. He is a freelance writer living in New York City. In the 1970s he self-published a book of poems called *Lost Blondes,* and in the years since a dozen or so other books (poems and novels) have come out from commercial presses. He has received grants and fellowships from the Guggenheim Foundation and the National Endowment for the Arts. He has taught at Princeton and the University of Alabama. W. W. Norton published his last poetry book, *Heroin and Other Poems,* in 2000 and will publish *Women of America* in early 2004. He is at work on a new novel, *As We Came from the Holy Land,* and a new book of poems, *Cosmopolis.*

Of "There's Trouble Everywhere," Smith writes: "I was walking up University Place, in New York City, early one morning when I saw a blind man (with his yellow Labrador guide dog) swaying ambivalently on a corner. I was struck by how even if the interesting young woman passing across the street was his long lost and daily grieved-over love he could not have spied her and rushed to greet her. It was so much like everybody's life in a way. At the typewriter one thing followed another. Little bits and tarted-up recollections slid into place along a line provided by attitude and tone. The young poet is someone I see around the Village, a performance artist, caught by glance as we passed each other on the stairs at our neighborhood theater, in person also unreachable."

MAURA STANTON was born in Evanston, Illinois, in 1946. She received her B.A. from the University of Minnesota and her MFA from the University of Iowa. Her first book of poetry, *Snow on Snow,* won the Yale Series of Younger Poets Award in 1975. Her second collection, *Cries of Swimmers,* was published by the University of Utah Press in 1984. (Both titles have been reprinted in the Carnegie Mellon Classic Contemporary Series.) *The Country I Come From,* stories about growing up in the Midwest, appeared from Milkweed Editions in 1988. Her other collections of stories include *Do Not Forsake Me, Oh My Darling* (University of Notre Dame Press) and the forthcoming *Cities in the Sea* (University of Michigan Press). She teaches at Indiana University and lives in Bloomington, Indiana.

Of "Translating," Stanton writes: "Sometimes you have to mix things up and invent a little to convey an experience in a poem. Here's the real story. One of my students had written a poem that used a number of Spanish words, so I went searching for my old *Cassell's Spanish Dictionary,* which I hadn't opened in years. I looked up his words, then began thumbing through the dictionary, reading here and there, fascinated by the definitions, surprised that many of them made no sense to me in English. I made a list of my favorites. As I began writing them out, doodling my way into a poem about them, I remembered that when my own novel, *Molly Companion,* was published in Spanish, I could barely read it. I also remembered my struggle to read a French novel last year, *Le Grand Meaulnes* by Alain Fournier. I wrote a line and discovered that I'd invented a novel in Spanish. And before I knew where the poem was headed, I'd placed the novel in a house I'd rented the summer before in Colorado, a summer when I'd been bored a lot, wishing I were in Europe. Once I had that dramatic situation set up, I also had a voice, located in space and time, that allowed me to express my delight in the words I'd found."

RUTH STONE was born in Roanoke, Virginia, in 1915. A professor in the English department at Binghamton University, she has received the Shelley Memorial Award, the National Book Critics Circle Award, two Guggenheim Fellowships, and the Wallace Stevens Prize from the Academy of American Poets. The most recent of her numerous books of poetry, *In the Next Galaxy* (Copper Canyon, 2002), won the National Book Award. She lives in a farmhouse in Vermont.

Of "Lines," Stone writes: "I was trying to describe how lines of poetry come to me. It seems like they come from way out in space and then move through me and go on. But of course they don't come from outside me, they're in my mind. The experience they refer to is outside me. After the lines come to me, I work on my poems to perfect them as much as possible. This poem is about that, the experience of inspiration."

JAMES TATE was born in Kansas City, Missouri, in 1943. His most recent book of poems, *Memoir of the Hawk,* was published by Ecco/Harper-Collins in 2001. Among his other books are *Shroud of the Gnome* (Ecco, 1997); *Worshipful Company of Fletchers* (Ecco, 1994), winner of the National Book Award; and *Selected Poems* (Wesleyan University Press, 1991), which received the Pulitzer Prize. *The Route as Briefed* appeared in the University of Michigan Press's Poets on Poetry Series in 1999. He teaches at the University of Massachusetts in Amherst and was the guest editor of *The Best American Poetry 1997.*

Tate writes: " 'The Restaurant Business' seems to me to be very much a slice of life—perhaps an exaggeration, but not too much. Some people say they hate their lives, and then will kill to defend them, because it's all they have, and they can't change. Their preposterous contradictions have achieved a perfect balance, and they don't really hurt anyone."

WILLIAM TREMBLAY was born in Southbridge, Massachusetts, in 1940. Among his seven collections of poetry are *Crying in the Cheap Seats* (University of Massachusetts Press, 1971), *Duhamel: Ideas of Order in Little Canada* (BOA Editions, 1987), *Rainstorm Over the Alphabet* (Lynx House Press, 2001), and the forthcoming *Door of Fire* (Eastern Washington University Press). For thirty years he has taught in the graduate writing program at Colorado State University. Recently he joined the Poudre Wilderness Volunteers, an auxiliary of the United States Forest Service, as a member of the trail crew and as an on-site teacher of "Leave No Trace" principles in the Canyon Lakes Ranger District, Colorado.

Tremblay writes: "The trail up Mt. Greyrock is steep in places. With hairpin switchbacks, hikers gain almost two thousand feet over three miles. As the title suggests, 'The Lost Boy' explores a parallel journey into the presence of absence. A stone monument at the trailhead reminds the speaker that the climb is dangerous and has claimed lives, especially of the young, who sometimes wander off from their families and are taken by wild animals or die of exhaustion, hypothermia, and starvation. Some remains are never found.

"The speaker first imagines a meeting with one boy's corpse. Then, as he continues, he takes on the weight of that death until it becomes his own, the death-in-life we all carry, the price of consciousness. The poem reaches the summit's granite heights and sees no end, but the speaker senses he's been changed by glimpsing a way to proceed."

NATASHA TRETHEWEY was born in Gulfport, Mississippi, in 1966. She is the author of *Bellocq's Ophelia* (Graywolf, 2002) and *Domestic Work* (Graywolf, 2000). She teaches English and creative writing at Emory University.

Of "After Your Death," Trethewey writes: "It's been almost twenty years since my mother's death, and yet the feeling of that loss sometimes reasserts itself, viscerally, as if the pain were still new and not simply filtered through the gauze of memory. For many years I had carried one of her large houseplants with me—moving from one apartment to the next, getting rid of other things that were hers, but not being able to part with this living thing she had touched. I was never good with it, and finally, it began to shrivel and die. It was a slow death, and I could see it coming in the leaves and the blackened stems. By then, I think, it was too late for me to save it, and I felt I was letting go of yet another part of her. This poem was a way for me, then, to grapple with the condition of loss and the space it creates, and to try, as I do over and over, filling that space with words."

DAVID WAGONER was born in Massillon, Ohio, in 1926. He has published seventeen books of poems, most recently *The House of Song* (University of Illinois Press, 2002), and ten novels, one of which, *The Escape Artist,* was made into a movie by Francis Ford Coppola in 1982. As editor of the Princeton University Press poetry series from 1978 to 1981, he chose the first books of Pattiann Rogers, Debora Greger, Robert Pinsky, Carl Dennis, and Jorie Graham. He was a chancellor of the Academy of American Poets for twenty-three years. He has taught at the University of Washington since 1954 and was the editor of *Poetry Northwest* until it ceased publication in 2002.

Of "On Being Asked to Discuss Poetic Theory," Wagoner writes: "I've often been asked to discuss poetic theory in public and in classes and have sometimes even done so voluntarily. Almost as often, I've been disappointed in or uneasy about what I've said. Whenever a categorical statement about poetry has come out of my mouth, a voice in my mind's ear has muttered, 'The opposite is just as true.' I think I wrote this poem because, instead of abstractions, I could use an analogy. So far, that voice hasn't been able to figure out what the opposite is."

RONALD WALLACE was born in Cedar Rapids, Iowa, in 1945, and grew up in St. Louis, Missouri. Since 1972 he has taught at the University of Wisconsin in Madison, where he is co-director of the creative writing program and editor of the University of Wisconsin Press poetry series. His twelve books of poetry, fiction, and criticism include *The Makings of Happiness* (1991), *Time's Fancy* (1994), *The Uses of Adversity* (1998), and *Long for This World: New and Selected Poems* (2003), all from the University of Pittsburgh Press. He divides his time between Madison and a forty-acre farm in Bear Valley, Wisconsin.

Wallace writes: "Humor has been a distinguishing characteristic of American poetry—from Dickinson and Whitman, through Frost, Stevens, Berryman, and others, down to the present—and I have done my best in my own work to carry on that tradition. Thus I was pleased when I found myself 'In a Rut,' with its comic narrative, its sexual banter, its double entendres, its playful repartee. When David Wagoner, himself a wonderful comic poet, accepted the poem for the final issue of *Poetry Northwest,* I was doubly pleased, and quickly sent the poem to Ed Ochester at the University of Pittsburgh Press for possible inclusion in *Long for This World: New and Selected Poems,* which was in the final stages of editing. Ed, who has been my friend and editor for years, and has always had an unerring eye for the strengths and weaknesses of my work, demurred. He left the decision to me, but suggested that the poem simply wasn't my best.

"I decided to test the poem on an audience. At a reading in the basement of a library in Marshfield, Wisconsin, I prefaced the poem by explaining my quandary and promising that I would let the audience decide the poem's fate. It was late in the reading, and I had established a rapport with the audience of about twenty-five people who seemed to like my work and to be enjoying themselves. I read the poem, spiritedly, jauntily. There were a few laughs, but at the end, a number of people (good-humoredly, I think) booed. When I asked why they had reacted in that way one woman said, 'I don't like wife-bashing.' 'Yikes!' I said, and tore up the poem on the spot, promising not to include it in my new book. My wife, Peg, who was sitting in the front row and hearing the poem for the first time (I had intended it as a kind of oddball love poem to her) later said she didn't think it was wife-bashing, but neither did she think it was particularly funny.

"So when I heard from David Lehman that Yusef Komunyakaa had selected 'In a Rut' for *The Best American Poetry,* my wife and I had to laugh. Here was that feisty poem again, giving us trouble and pleasure. Giving us what, perhaps, after all, the best humor and poetry must."

LEWIS WARSH was born in New York City in 1944. His books include *Ted's Favorite Skirt* (Spuyten Duyvil, 2002), *The Origin of the World* (Creative Arts, 2001), *Touch of the Whip* (Singing Horse, 2001), *Debtor's Prison,* a collaboration with Julie Harrison (Granary, 2001), and *Money Under the Table* (Trip Street Books, 1997). He is co-editor, with Anne Waldman, of *The Angel Hair Anthology* (Granary, 2001). A double CD of a live reading of *The Origin of the World* appeared in 2003 from Deerhead Records. He is editor and publisher of United Artists Books and teaches in the English department of Long Island University in Brooklyn.

Warsh writes: "I put together 'Premonition' in January 2001. I was living in Greenpoint, Brooklyn, not far from the East River. I wrote the next-to-last section and then all the other poems and fragments of poems suddenly made sense to me. Many of the other sections had been written years or months earlier. The 'hotel on Broadway' refers to the Dante in San Francisco."

SUSAN WHEELER was born in Pittsburgh, Pennsylvania, in 1955. Her first collection of poetry, *Bag 'o' Diamonds,* published in 1993 by the University of Georgia Press, received the Norma Farber First Book Award of the Poetry Society of America. Her second, *Smokes,* won the Four Way Books Award in 1998, and her third, *Source Codes,* was published by SALT Publishing in 2001. Her work has appeared in six editions of *The Best American Poetry.* She is on the creative writing faculties at Princeton University and the New School, and lives in New York City.

Wheeler writes: " 'In Sky' was written to accompany paintings by Susanna Coffey. They are extraordinary self-portraits, although their true subject is the relationship of figure to ground, lyrics to music, interiority to exteriority, etc., all intensified by the pressure of self. This particular series was keyed to blue, blue infusing the paintings with titles like 'With Mariposa,' 'Bay,' 'IC! Berlin,' and 'Masque Queen Hélène.' The heads in the pictures work as metaphors, working with and against abstraction, and answer what Susanna calls the 'mortal wound around figure painting,' spun in part from the particular tradition of male painters and female models."

RICHARD WILBUR was born in New York City in 1921. He attended Amherst College and served, during World War II, with the 36th Infantry Division. He retired from academic life in 1986, having taught at Harvard, Wellesley, Wesleyan, and Smith; he and his wife now divide their time between Cummington, Massachusetts, and Key West, Florida. His latest book of poems, *Mayflies,* was published by Harcourt in 2000. His translations of Molière and Racine, also published by Harcourt, are widely performed, and 2003 saw a major production of *Tartuffe* on Broadway.

Of "Man Running," Wilbur writes: "I've always been intrigued by the doubleness of our feelings about fugitives from justice. There is in each of us a frightened Hobbesian who desires, above everything, the enforcement of order. Yet most of us are half-inclined—through compassion, or romantic individualism, or some ancient solidarity—to root for any man who is in flight from the authorities, and hope that he will get away.

"Such feelings do not, in any case, extend to the mass murderer

Osama bin Laden, as one reader of *The New Yorker*, who wrote me from Miami, thought they might."

C. K. WILLIAMS was born in Newark, New Jersey, in 1936. His most recent books of poetry are *The Vigil* (1997) and *Repair* (1999), which won the Pulitzer Prize, both published by Farrar, Straus and Giroux, and a collection of his poems on love, *Love About Love* (Ausable Press, 2001). He is also the author of a book of essays, *Poetry and Consciousness* (University of Michigan Press, 1998), and *Misgivings* (Farrar, Straus and Giroux, 2000), a book of autobiographical meditation. He has recently completed a play, *Operations,* and his new book of poems, *The Singing,* will be published in fall 2003. He teaches in the writing program at Princeton University.

Of "The World," Williams writes: "I write this in January 2003, waiting for the onset of a seemingly inevitable, reckless, utterly unnecessary war, and for the disasters which will surely ensue from it. In a time of such harrowing anxiety, it seems almost impossible to re-live that moment, such a short year and a half ago, when 'The World' was written, when something like uncomplicated well-being, not to say bliss, could be experienced, however briefly.

"I have to admit that I wouldn't have used the word 'bliss' even then; I don't think it's a word I've ever attached to my own life, perhaps out of some old superstition about offending the furies of chance. But the poem does embody for me something like felicity, in the effortless flow of reality through me I felt that afternoon, and in the surge of a poem getting under way, when so many seemingly disparate perceptions and reflections are all at once welded together, in what I suppose has to be called inspiration. I think I long now toward those minutes then hours and days of the poem's composition and revision, when the linkages of the private and public domains weren't so fraught as they are now, when a newspaper could be a source of aesthetic curiosity, rather than political dread.

"This sounds terribly gloomy. I wish it didn't have to be. I wish I could think again of the world as the benevolent place it was that day, not the one I tremble in now. I wish I didn't have to write this."

TERENCE WINCH was born in the Bronx, New York, on All Saints' Day, 1945. He stayed there until 1971, when he moved to Washington, D.C. He made a living writing and playing traditional Irish music until 1985, when he got a regular job as an editor at a museum. One of his songs, "When New York Was Irish," has become something of a standard in certain music circles. His most recent books of poems are *The Drift of Things* (The Figures, 2001) and *The Great Indoors* (Story Line Press, 1995). Hanging Loose Press is bringing out a book of his nonfiction stories in late 2003, and he has also completed a novel for young readers. He has released several recordings—as composer, musician, and producer—with Celtic Thunder.

Of "My Work," Winch writes: "A few years ago, I took part in a group reading in D.C. One of my fellow poets, a young writer who was just starting out, introduced each of his poems by quoting parts of a laudatory essay about his work that he himself had written. I thought: What a great idea for a poem. Not long after, I wrote 'My Work.' In the last stanza, there's a bit of an echo of the famous speech from the dock by Irish patriot Robert Emmet, who was executed by the British in 1803. I had memorized the speech in high school."

DAVID WOJAHN was born in St. Paul, Minnesota, in 1953. He is the author of six collections of poetry, most recently *The Falling Hour* (1997) and *Spirit Cabinet* (2002), both from the University of Pittsburgh Press. He is also the author of a collection of essays on contemporary poetry, *Strange Good Fortune* (University of Arkansas Press, 2001). He has received two fellowships from the National Endowment for the Arts, the Amy Lowell Traveling Poetry Scholarship, the Yale Younger Poets Prize, and the William Carlos Williams Book Award. He is a professor of English at Virginia Commonwealth University and a faculty member in the graduate writing program at Vermont College.

Wojahn writes: "'Scrabble with Matthews' is an elegy for William Matthews, who died in 1997. His poetry has meant a great deal to me over the years, and I especially value its wit, tonal authority, and intimacy. He was a marvelously erudite poet, but he wore his learning casually. The dramatic situation of the poem—playing Scrabble with Matthews in the bar of a snowbound airport—is partly true but mostly fiction. The statements about poetry that Matthews makes to the students are quoted verbatim, however. The poem also derives from an exercise I gave myself: I wanted to find a plausible context for a short list of highly arcane words that you wouldn't expect to encounter in a poem. Thus you have 'jerboa,' 'phalanx' and 'qintar.' The latter word, which Matthews knows but the speaker doesn't, is a term you'd employ only if you were an expert Scrabble player. It's one of the handful of English words that begin with 'q' and don't need a 'u' to follow it. A 'bingo' in Scrabble occurs when a player uses all seven of his or her letters. 'Endquote' played over two 'triple word scores' would yield the player a staggering 182 points."

ROBERT WRIGLEY was born in East St. Louis, Illinois, in 1951. He is a professor of English and director of the graduate program in creative writing at the University of Idaho. He has published six books of poems, including *In the Bank of Beautiful Sins* (Penguin, 1995) and *Reign of Snakes* (Penguin, 1999), which was awarded the 2000 Kingsley Tufts Award. His new book, in which "Clemency" appears, is *Lives of the Animals* (Penguin, 2003).

Wrigley writes: "Like the weather that triggered it, and which it means to describe, 'Clemency' felt like a gift: it came swiftly and easily one afternoon, so easily, in fact, that I did not trust it much and left it scrawled in pencil in my notebook for nearly two years. The day I wrote it, mid-February 1998, I'd gone out at midday to grain the horses, and I didn't even wear a coat. This is in north Idaho, where that otherwise truncated month usually seems a winter's length all by itself. I was as skeptical of the weather as I would be of the poem that came from it. What changed my mind about the poem, when I rediscovered it years later, was the quirky language as much as anything: 'whistly,' for example; or the polysyllables, like 'scintillate,' 'bedeviled,' 'garlanded,' and 'garrulous'; even the Donne pun. I believe the miraculous weather that day made itself felt in the poem via a sort of linguistic exuberance, and I believe that exuberant language allowed me the poem's simple, prayerful, and bodily final two lines, which, if I am lucky, are as much about the ache of blessings as about the benediction."

ANNA ZIEGLER was born in New York City in 1979. She graduated from Yale University in 2001 and received a master's degree in creative writing (poetry) from the University of East Anglia, in Norwich, England, in 2002. She is an editorial assistant at *The Saint Ann's Review* and a graduate student in the MFA program in dramatic writing at NYU.

Of "After the Opening, 1932," Ziegler writes: "I love the work of Edward Hopper and have written poems in the past inspired by the narratives suggested in his paintings. This time, I wanted to write a narrative of Hopper himself. I imagined a fanciful moment in which he understood that he could go further with the idea of life's emptiness in his work, that this would speak to even greater truths, among them that every piece of art implies a sort of absence—that of the artist having left it behind, the way, in the poem, he has left his Opening and moved on."

AHMOS ZU-BOLTON II was born in Mississippi in 1946. He is the author of five books of poetry: *A Niggered Amen* (Solo Press, 1975), *Stumbling Thru: earth(ing)poems* (Energy BlackSouth/Energy Earth Communications, 1981), *a sneak preview* (Copastetic Books, 1992), *Ain't No Spring Chicken* (Voice Foundation, 1998), and *1946* (Ishmael Reed Publishing Company, 2002). His forthcoming book is *Every Once in a Long While*. He is currently visiting writer-in-residence at the University of Missouri.

MAGAZINES WHERE THE POEMS
WERE FIRST PUBLISHED

American Poetry Review, eds. Stephen Berg, David Bonanno, and Arthur Vogelsgang. 1721 Walnut Street, Philadelphia, Pennsylvania 19103.

Barrow Street, eds. Patricia Carlin, Peter Covino, Lois Hirschkowitz, and Melissa Hotchkiss. PO Box 2017, Old Chelsea Station, New York, New York 10113.

BOMB, ed. Betsy Sussler. 594 Broadway, Suite 905, New York, New York 10012.

Boston Review, poetry eds. Mary Jo Bang and Timothy Donnelly. E53-407, MIT, 30 Wadsworth Street, Cambridge, Massachusetts 02139-4307.

Brilliant Corners, ed. Sascha Feinstein. Lycoming College, Williamsport, Pennsylvania 17701.

Callaloo, ed. Charles H. Rowell. Department of English, Texas A&M University, Blocker 249, TAMU 4227, College Station, Texas 77843.

Colorado Review, poetry eds. Jorie Graham and Donald Revell. Dept. of English, Colorado State University, Ft. Collins, Colorado 80523.

Croonenbergh's Fly, ed. Philip Connors. 3410 33rd St., #4B, Astoria, New York 11106.

88, ed. Ian Randall Wilson. PO Box 2872, Venice, California 90294.

Field, Oberlin College, eds. Pamela Alexander, Martha Collins, David Walker, and David Young. 10 N. Professor St., Oberlin, Ohio 44074.

Five Points, eds. David Bottoms and Megan Sexton. Georgia State University, 33 Gilmer St. S.E., Unit 8, Atlanta, Georgia 30303-3088.

Gargoyle, eds. Lucinda Ebersole and Richard Peabody. PO Box 6216, Arlington, Virginia 22206-0216.

Harper's Magazine, ed. Lewis H. Lapham. 666 Broadway, New York, New York 10012.

The Kenyon Review, ed. David Lynn. Walton House, Kenyon College, Gambier, Ohio 43022.

London Review of Books, ed. Mary-Kay Wilmers. 28 Little Russell Street, London, WC1A 2HN, United Kingdom.

LUNA, ed. Ray Gonzalez. English Department, University of Minnesota, 207 Lind Hall, 207 Church St., Minneapolis, Minnesota 55455.

Mid-American Review, poetry ed. Karen Craigo. Department of English, Bowling Green State University, Bowling Green, Ohio 43403.

Mississippi Review, poetry ed. Angela Ball. University of Southern Mississippi, Box 5144, Hattiesburg, Mississippi 39406-5144.

New American Writing, eds. Paul Hoover and Maxine Chernoff. 369 Molino Avenue, Mill Valley, California 94941.

New England Review, poetry ed. C. Dale Young. Middlebury College, Middlebury, Vermont 05753.

The New York Review of Books, eds. Robert B. Silvers and Barbara Epstein. 1755 Broadway, 5th Floor, New York, New York 10019.

The New Yorker, poetry ed. Alice Quinn. 4 Times Square, New York, New York 10036.

Ontario Review, eds. Raymond J. Smith and Joyce Carol Oates. 9 Honey Brook Drive, Princeton, New Jersey 08540.

The Paris Review, poetry ed. Richard Howard. 541 East 72 Street, New York, New York 10021.

Pleiades, poetry ed. Kevin Prufer. Department of English and Philosophy, Central Missouri State University, Warrensburg, Missouri 64093.

Ploughshares, poetry ed. David Daniel. Emerson College, 100 Beacon St., Boston, Massachusetts 02116.

PMS, ed. Linda Frost. University of Alabama at Birmingham, Department of English, 217 Humanities Building, 900 South 13th St., Birmingham, Alabama 35294-1260.

Poetry, ed. Joseph Parisi. 60 W. Walton St., Chicago, Illinois 60610-3380.

Poetry Daily, eds. Rob Anderson, Diane Boller, and Don Selby. www.poems.com.

Poetry Northwest, ed. David Wagoner. Box 354330, University of Washington, Seattle, Washington 98195.

The Poetry Project Newsletter, ed. Ange Mlinko. St. Mark's Church, 131 E. 10th St., New York, New York 10003.

The Progressive, ed. Matthew Rothschild. 409 East Main St., Madison, Wisconsin 53703.

Rattapallax, poetry ed. Martin Mitchell. 532 La Guardia Place, Suite 353, New York, New York 10012.

Rattle, poetry ed. Stellasue Lee. 13440 Ventura Blvd. #200, Sherman Oaks, California 91423.

Rhino, eds. Deborah Nodler Rosen, Alice George, Kathleen Kirk, and Helen Degen Cohen. PO Box 591, Evanston, Illinois 60204.

Spinning Jenny, ed. C. E. Harrison. Black Dress Press, PO Box 1373, New York, New York 10276.

Spoon River Poetry Review, ed. Lucia Cordell Getsi. 4240 Department of English, Illinois State University, Normal, Illinois 61790-4240.

Third Coast, poetry eds. Richard Foss, Kirsten Hemmy, and Billy Reynolds. Department of English, Western Michigan University, Kalamazoo, Michigan 49008-5092.

The Threepenny Review, poetry ed. Wendy Lesser. PO Box 9131, Berkeley, California 94709.

Tin House, poetry ed. Amy Bartlett. 2601 NW Thurman St., Portland, Oregon 97210.

TriQuarterly, ed. Susan Firestone Hahn. 2020 Ridge Ave., Evanston, Illinois 60208-4302.

Verse, eds. Brian Henry and Andrew Zawacki. English Department, University of Georgia, Athens, Georgia, 30602.

Washington Post Magazine, ed. Tom Shroder. 1150 15th Street, NW, Washington, D.C. 20071.

Witness, ed. Peter Stine. 27055 Orchard Lake Road, Farmington Hills, Michigan 48334.

The World, ed. Ed Friedman. The Poetry Project, St. Mark's Church, 131 E. 10th St., New York, New York 10003.

ACKNOWLEDGMENTS

The series editor wishes to thank Mark Bibbins for his invaluable assistance. Ideas or suggestions from Angela Ball, Shanna Compton, Stacey Harwood, Danielle Pafunda, Carly Sachs, Michael Schiavo, and Susan Wheeler were greatly appreciated. Warm thanks go also to Glen Hartley and Lynn Chu, of Writers' Representatives, and to Rachel Sussman, Erin Curler, Cristine LeVasser, and Erich Hobbing at Scribner.

Grateful acknowledgment is made of the magazines in which these poems first appeared and the magazine editors who selected them. Unless otherwise noted, copyright to the poems is held by the individual poets.

Jonathan Aaron: "The End of *Out of the Past*" appeared in *London Review of Books*. Reprinted by permission of the poet.

Beth Anderson: from "A Locked Room" appeared in *The Poetry Project Newsletter*. Reprinted by permission of the poet.

Nin Andrews: "Dedicated to the One I Love" from *Why They Grow Wings*. Copyright © 2000 by Nin Andrews. Reprinted by permission of the poet and Silverfish Press. Also appeared in *Gargoyle*.

Wendell Berry: "Some Further Words" appeared in *American Poetry Review*. Reprinted by permission of the poet.

Frank Bidart: "Curse" appeared in *The Threepenny Review*. Reprinted by permission of the poet.

Diann Blakely: "Rambling on My Mind" appeared in *BOMB*. Reprinted by permission of the poet.

Bruce Bond: "Art Tatum" appeared in *The Paris Review*. Reprinted by permission of the poet.

Catherine Bowman: from "1000 Lines," appeared in *TriQuarterly*. Reprinted by permission of the poet.

Rosemary Catacalos: "Perfect Attendance: Short Subjects Made from the Staring Photos of Strangers" appeared in *The Progressive*. Reprinted by permission of the poet.

Joshua Clover: "Aeon Flux: June" appeared in *Ploughshares*. Reprinted by permission of the poet.

Billy Collins: "Litany" appeared in *Poetry,* copyright © 2002 by Billy